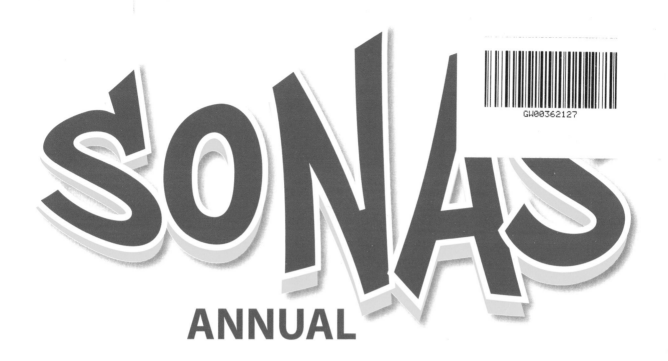

# SONAS
## ANNUAL

CELEBRATING New Year!

TOP 10 Christmas MOVIES

SARAH WEBB

INTERVIEWS

Dinny Corcoran

50

MOON Landing

Ireland's HOCKEY TEAM

FOLENS

ISBN: 978-1-78927-915-3

© Folens Publishers 2019
Hibernian Industrial Estate
Greenhills Road
Tallaght
Dublin 24

| | |
|---|---|
| **Design:** | Lovatts Media |
| **Illustrators:** | Luke Gallaway, Andrew Coppard, Rhiannon Ryder, Sinéad Woods and Úna Woods (Baboom Design) |
| **Photos:** | Shutterstock, Wikimedia Commons, Inpho Photography, Alamy, Rolling News, Ger Holland, Sandra Mailer, Independent News & Media. |
| **Copyright material:** | Reprinted by kind permission of The O'Brien Press Ltd., Dublin: p. 20: Cover of *Dare to Dream: Irish People Who Took on the World (and Won!)* by Sarah Webb. Illustrated by Graham Corcoran, 2019. p. 21: Cover of *A Sailor Went to Sea, Sea, Sea* by Sarah Webb. Illustrated by Steve McCarthy, 2017; Cover of *Blazing a Trail: Irish Women Who Changed the World* by Sarah Webb. Illustrated by Lauren O'Neill, 2018. |
| | Reprinted by kind permission of Walker Books Ltd., London: p. 22: Cover of *The Songbird Cafe Girls: Aurora and the Popcorn Dolphin* by Sarah Webb, 2016; Cover of *The Songbird Cafe Girls: Sunny Days and Moon Cakes* by Sarah Webb, 2015. |
| **Articles:** | 'Top 10 Christmas Movies' by Chris Galvin; 'Swimming in a Sea of Plastic' by Louise Merrigan; 'The Late Late Toy Show', 'Crazy Brain Facts', '50th Anniversary of the Moon Landing', 'World Cup Silver Medallists – Ireland's Hockey Team' and 'Happy New Year!' by Natasha Mac a'Bháird. |
| **Quizzes:** | 'Book Quiz' and 'The Sports Quiz' by Natasha Mac a'Bháird; 'Cracking Christmas Quiz' by Chris Galvin; 'Fact or Fiction' by Louise Merrigan. |
| **Recipes:** | Louise Merrigan |
| **All other editorial content:** | Lynn Fitzpatrick except 'Writing Time' by Natasha Mac a'Bháird |
| **Contributors:** | A big thank you to Sarah Webb and Dinny Corcoran for talking to us about their careers so far. |

**A huge thank you and congratulations to the following readers for their fantastic contributions to this annual:**

| | |
|---|---|
| **Stories:** | Oliver Schuch, Caoimhe Flannery |
| **Facts/Jokes/Tongue-Twisters:** | Alex Peters, Caoimhe McKeogh, Caoimhe Ahern, Dayna Duffy, Hannah Lucey and Anna Johnston |

**We look forward to receiving lots more fantastic stories, jokes, tongue-twisters and other contributions in 2020!**

**Lovatts** CROSSWORDS&PUZZLES Puzzle Content © Lovatts Media 2019.

# WHAT'S INSIDE...

**SAY NO** TO SINGLE-USE PLASTIC

## PLUS!

## AS GAEILGE!

## AND LOTS MORE!

# Word Games

## Last Word Standing

Use the clues to cross out the words in the boxes. One word will be left over.
This last word standing is the mystery answer.

**Clues:**

- All colours in a rainbow
- All breakfast foods
- All types of exercise
- All items in a schoolbag
- All words with 'M' as the second letter
- All things you'll find at the beach
- All words that rhyme with 'best'
- All numbers under twenty

| | | |
|---|---|---|
| CLIMBING | | SEASHELLS |
| TEN | SAND | PANCAKES |
| CEREAL | GREEN | NEST |
| REST | PEST | WALKING |
| BLUE | SWIMMING | THREE |
| SALTWATER | TOAST | ERASERS |
| EMPTY | SMART | YELLOW |
| BOOKS | PENCILS | HOLIDAY |
| FIFTEEN | | UMPIRE |

## Chainletters

Can you find the 13-letter word hiding in the chain?
You must use all 13 letters once only and you can move from circle to circle but only where they are connected by lines.

## What's What

Complete the three-letter words, and the middle row across will reveal the solution

| 1 | 2 | 3 | 4 | 5 | 6 | 7 | 8 |
|---|---|---|---|---|---|---|---|
| A | E | J | A | M | O | G | P |
| | | | | | | | |
| C | F | G | H | G | F | N | Y |

1. Alphabet (1,1,1)
2. Santa's helper
3. Irish dance
4. Fire remains
5. Food enhancer (1,1,1)
6. ... the beaten track
7. Marksman's tool
8. Tissue layer

4

# Cé mhéad?

Cé mhéad de gach rud atá sa phictiúr?
Scríobh an uimhir cheart sa bhosca.

 Piongain ar dhréimire

 Piongain ag déanamh lámhchleasaíocht

 Sionnach ina chodladh

 Iasc oráiste

# TOP 10
# Christmas Movies

The Christmas holidays just wouldn't feel complete without Christmas movies. But with so many festive flicks to choose from, which ones should you watch? We have whittled down our favourites to come up with the ultimate Top 10 list. Read on to see if any of your top picks made the cut!

## 10 Jingle All the Way (1996)

It's Christmas Eve and the Langston family are all set for Christmas, except Howard (Arnold Schwarzenegger). Howard hasn't been around much for his son, Jamie, and he wants to make it up to him. He promises to get Jamie a present of Turbo-Man, the hottest new toy in shops. There's just one problem: Turbo-Man is almost sold out! Howard will need to resort to some desperate and hilarious measures if he wants to get his hands on the toy in time for Christmas!

## 9 The Christmas Chronicles (2018)

Kate and Teddy Pierce plan to capture Santa Claus on Christmas Eve. But when they do catch up with him, they jeopardise Christmas for everyone. With plenty of crazy adventures, and Kurt Russell taking on the role of jolly Saint Nick, *The Christmas Chronicles* is a fun movie with a lot of belly laughs.

## 8 Arthur Christmas (2011)

On Christmas Eve, Santa delivers presents to every boy and girl in the world. What people don't know is that this has become a high-tech operation where every present is delivered with precision timing. That is, until one present goes astray, and Santa's youngest son, Arthur, resolves to deliver it before Christmas morning. This film offers a unique take on the story of Santa's workshop, with stunning animation, good humour and lots of heart.

## 7 The Grinch (2018)

The Whos of Whoville love Christmas. Their town is a festive wonderland of colour, gifts and lights. But not everyone is in the mood to celebrate, especially the Grinch who lives in a cave near the top of Mount Crumpit. The Grinch hates Christmas. He hates it so much he plans to steal it. But how can you steal Christmas? Watch this animated adventure to find out!

## 6 It's a Wonderful Life (1946)

George Bailey is having a terrible Christmas Eve. He feels as though his life has been one inconvenience after another, and now his business is about to collapse. Just when George is giving up all hope, he meets an angel named Clarence. Clarence gives George a new perspective, by showing him what life would have been like for everyone George knows and loves, if George had never been born. *It's a Wonderful Life* is a Christmas classic with a life-affirming message.

**5**

### Miracle on 34th Street (1994)

Susan Walker is six years old and she doesn't believe in Santa Claus. That is, until a kindly, old man by the name of Kris Kringle becomes the Santa for Cole's Department Store (where Susan's mother works). Kris has a big white beard, an impressive suit and he can talk to reindeer. Could he be the real deal? The only way to know for sure is to watch this Christmas classic!

**2**

### Elf (2003)

When Buddy the Elf makes the startling discovery that he is not an elf, he travels to New York to find his human father. In New York, Buddy discovers a strange new world that could definitely use a little Christmas spirit. The actor Will Ferrell plays Buddy with an infectious glee and joy that borders on crazy – but nonetheless the character is highly endearing. This is a hilarious movie with a lot of heart.

**1**

### The Muppet Christmas Carol (1992)

There have been numerous adaptations of Charles Dickens's classic *A Christmas Carol* – but the Muppet version is our favourite take on this tale. The film balances the spooky story of a miser visited by three ghosts, with humour and songs that will stay with you long after the movie ends. Michael Caine plays a fantastic Scrooge, while Gonzo, Rizzo the Rat, Miss Piggy and Kermit the Frog provide plenty of laughs. *The Muppet Christmas Carol* is all about the true meaning of Christmas spirit and that's why it earned its place in the number one spot!

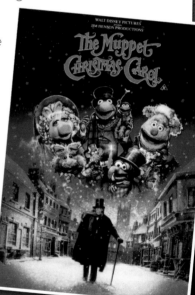

**4**

### The Nightmare Before Christmas (1993)

Jack Skellington, the leader of Halloween Town, is weary from organising Halloween celebrations every year. When he stumbles across Christmas Town, he decides he wants to take over Christmas! Will anyone be able to stop Jack before he realises what a terrible mistake he's making? Full of toe-tapping songs and incredible stop-motion animation, *The Nightmare Before Christmas* is a Christmas film with a spooky twist.

**3**

### Home Alone (1990)

What would you do if you woke up to find your whole family had disappeared? If you're Kevin McCallister, you celebrate! After a horrible fight with his mother, Kevin wishes his whole family would go away. When he wakes the next morning, they're gone! Kevin's initial celebratory mood is cut short by the arrival of 'The Wet Bandits'. The Bandits are a pair of bumbling crooks who make several attempts to break into the McCallister home, believing it to be empty. Kevin takes extraordinary and creative measures to fend off the bandits! With plenty of slapstick humour, *Home Alone* is a laugh-a-minute family favourite.

**ADMIT** 5004 50

#### Honourable mentions

Here are some classic Christmas movies that just missed out on our list. These are definitely worth a watch!

- *A Christmas Story (1983)*
- *Gremlins (1984)*
- *Home Alone 2: Lost in New York (1992)*
- *The Santa Clause (1994)*
- *Jack Frost (1998)*

# Bake It!

**Contains nuts!**

## Spritzgebäck Biscuit Decorations

Ask an adult to help you make these delicious German Christmas biscuits. You will need two baking trays lined with greaseproof paper. Preheat the oven to 180°C/Gas Mark 4.

## Ingredients:

- 380 g butter, softened
- 250 g golden caster sugar
- A few drops of vanilla extract
- A pinch of salt
- 500 g plain flour
- 125 g ground almonds

## To decorate:

- 100 g dark chocolate
- Colourful ribbons or string

**1** In a large bowl, mix the butter, sugar, vanilla extract and salt. Gradually add two-thirds of the flour, mixing in a little at a time.

**2** Mix in the rest of the flour and the ground almonds. Tip the mixture onto a clean work surface and knead for a few minutes.

**3** Shape the dough into smooth rolls. Join the ends to form circles. Place on the baking trays.

**Tip:** Smooth the circles at the join – this ensures they won't break apart when baked.

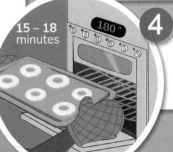

15 – 18 minutes

**4** Place the biscuits on the baking tray. Bake for 15–18 minutes until lightly golden.

**5** Gently remove the biscuits to a wire rack to cool.

**6** Break the chocolate into pieces and gently melt it in a bowl in the microwave. Dip the cooled biscuits in the melted chocolate, one by one. Dip one end only – then return the biscuit to the wire rack to set.

**Tip:** Tie ribbon or string through the centre of the biscuits to create beautiful Christmas decorations.

# Christmas Time

Find all the items pictured, and cross them off in the grid of letters. The leftover letters will reveal the mystery answer.

| S | A | W | B | A | U | B | L | E | H |
|---|---|---|---|---|---|---|---|---|---|
| N | T | G | R | E | L | D | N | A | C |
| R | H | G | I | E | L | S | T | L | A |
| R | E | N | N | F | A | L | C | E | L |
| S | E | I | A | I | T | T | S | G | Y |
| T | R | K | N | M | D | S | H | N | L |
| H | T | C | C | D | W | D | A | A | L |
| G | W | O | B | A | E | O | U | U | O |
| I | S | T | A | R | R | E | N | P | H |
| L | E | S | N | I | T | C | R | S | S |

MYSTERY ANSWER:

# THE LATE LATE TOY SHOW

Put on your favourite pyjamas, grab your treats, pick a spot on the couch. It's time for *The Late Late Toy Show*! This magical TV show marks the start of the Christmas season for many families all over Ireland. It's been a special tradition for parents and children to watch it together for over 40 years! Smaller children often watch it the next day, or fall asleep after 10 minutes, so it's a proper milestone when you're allowed to stay up and watch the whole show for the very first time.

## Where it all began

*The Late Late Show* is the longest-running talk show in the whole world! Its original host was Gay Byrne, and one of his researchers suggested doing a special slot on toys for Christmas. The feature was such a success that the producers decided to expand the idea into a whole show about toys, and it quickly became an Irish institution!

As one of the best-known presenters on Irish television, Gay Byrne normally tackled quite serious issues and always wore a suit. But, for *The Toy Show*, he felt free to be as silly as he liked, wearing a Christmas jumper and rolling around on the floor with the children.

When Gay retired, Pat Kenny took over. One of the key changes he made to the show was to make a dramatic entrance. One time, he rolled onto the set in a giant zorbing ball and another time he jumped out of a helicopter! But his own favourite moment was when he got to ride into the studio on an elephant!

The current presenter is Ryan Tubridy, who says *The Toy Show* is his favourite programme of the year.

## The grand opening

With Ryan Tubridy as host, *The Toy Show* opens with a song and dance routine from well-known films. Ryan has appeared on stage dressed as Sebastian the lobster from *The Little Mermaid*, Woody from *Toy Story*, Baloo from *The Jungle Book* and Willy Wonka.

In 2017, a new film was released which quickly became a firm favourite with families all over Ireland – that's right, *The Greatest Showman*!

Ryan himself is a huge fan of this film, so it was chosen as the theme for the 2018 *Toy Show*. Ryan played the role of P.T. Barnum in the opening number, making a dramatic entrance in the middle of a circus ring with a chorus of children dressed as the much-loved characters from the film, including the bearded lady, stilt-walkers and acrobats. The theme featured throughout the show, with many of the most popular songs being sung by the talented child performers.

What will the opening of this year's *Toy Show* be like? We can't wait to find out!

## Magical moments

Over the years there have been many truly magical moments on the *Toy Show*. Brother and sister Kayla and Adam were chatting to Ryan about some toys they had tried out when he asked them about their father. Adam explained that he was a soldier serving with the United Nations in Mali, and they hadn't seen him in six months. But there was a surprise in store. When Ryan got the children to unwrap a giant box, their dad jumped out! There were tears of joy all round as they were joined onstage by their mum and younger sister, Emily. The family were thrilled to be back together for Christmas.

The heart-warming story of another special family really touched the nation. Eight-year-old Scott appeared on the show to surprise his mother and aunt, who were in the audience. Scott's cousin, six-year-old Grace, had been ill with leukaemia. Brave Scott donated bone marrow that helped to save her life. The entire family then appeared on the show, and Ryan presented them with a special prize of a trip to Florida. There wasn't a dry eye in the house!

## What does 2019 have in store?

The theme of the *Toy Show* is always top-secret until the day of the show, and as for surprise guests, star performers and audience giveaways – you'll just have to watch to find out!

### *The Toy Show* 2018 in numbers!

**1.5 million:** Viewers who watched the show in 2018, making it the most popular show of the year in Ireland.

**109:** Countries worldwide where the show was watched.

**222:** Toys featured.

**200:** Child performers.

**30:** Child demonstrators.

**140,000:** People who applied for audience tickets.

**204:** The number who were successful in getting tickets.

# Phone Code

Stephen is texting his friend a riddle. Can you work out what it is?
Use the mobile phone keypad to crack the code.
Each number in the riddle represents one of the letters on that key on the phone.
Remember: You need to work out which letter it is and it's not always the same letter.

9428 36 732
66678377 328?
3474 263
74477!

___ ___ __ ___

_____ _____ ___ ___?

___ __ ___

____!

# Word Pairs

Match the word pairs to find seven things relating to Christmas. One word will be left over. This is the mystery answer.

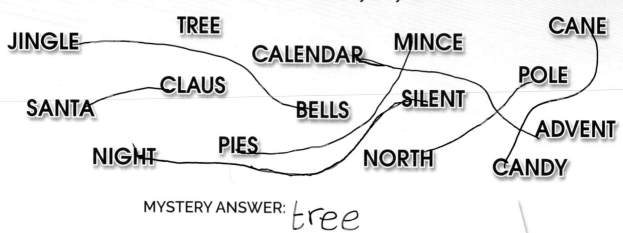

JINGLE  TREE  CALENDAR  MINCE  CANE
CLAUS  POLE
SANTA  BELLS  SILENT
PIES  ADVENT
NIGHT  NORTH  CANDY

MYSTERY ANSWER: *tree*

# Colour Sudoku

Fill in the missing numbers so that numbers 1–9 occur only once in each row (going across), each column (going down) and each 3 x 3 box. In this puzzle there are also nine different colours, each with nine squares, and the numbers 1–9 must appear only once in each colour.

# FACT OR FICTION

Can you work out which of the following are fact and which are fiction?

1. Reindeer hooves expand in summer when the ground is soft, and shrink in winter when the ground is hard.

☐ FACT ☐ FICTION

2. The first *Late Late Toy Show* was broadcast in 1958.

☐ FACT ☐ FICTION

3. The African continent is larger than Australia, Canada and the USA combined.

☐ FACT ☐ FICTION

4. Wicklow is known as the 'Garden of Ireland'.

☐ FACT ☐ FICTION

5. Saffron is the world's most expensive spice.

☐ FACT ☐ FICTION

6. Istanbul is the capital of Turkey.

☐ FACT ☐ FICTION

7. The Rubik's cube was first named 'The Impossible Cube'.

☐ FACT ☐ FICTION

8. Chelsea, Arsenal and Crystal Palace are all football clubs based in London.

☐ FACT ☐ FICTION

9. The Swahili word 'safari' means 'holiday'.
☐ FACT ☐ FICTION

10. Planet Mars is named after the Roman god of war.
☐ FACT ☐ FICTION

11. An Irish Wolfhound holds the Guinness World Record for the tallest dog in the world.
☐ FACT ☐ FICTION

12. Acrophobia is an extreme fear of heights.
☐ FACT ☐ FICTION

13. A group of giraffes is called a herd.
☐ FACT ☐ FICTION

14. Judo originated in Japan.
☐ FACT ☐ FICTION

15. Dublin Zoo is the oldest zoo in the world.
☐ FACT ☐ FICTION

16. 'Áras an Uachtaráin' means 'The White House' in Irish.
☐ FACT ☐ FICTION

17. Ireland has more kilometres of motorway than New Zealand.
☐ FACT ☐ FICTION

18. Louth is the smallest county in Ireland.
☐ FACT ☐ FICTION

19. A pumpkin is a fruit.
☐ FACT ☐ FICTION

20. O'Shea is Ireland's most common surname.
☐ FACT ☐ FICTION

# Irish Word Match

How much Christmas vocabulary do you know in Irish? Match up the correct translation for each Irish word, then check the Solutions page to see how many you got right: 12–16 is excellent, 8–11 is very good and less than 8 means there is room for improvement.

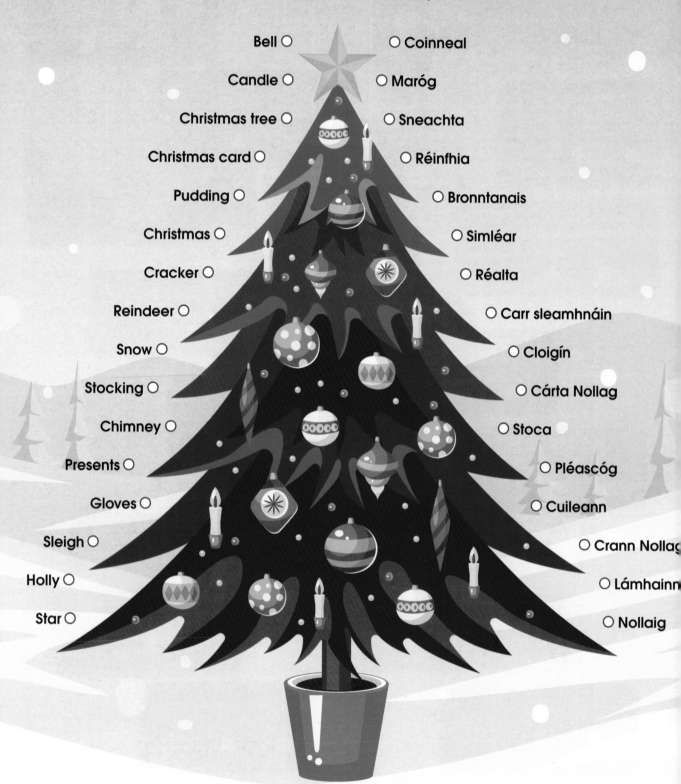

| | |
|---|---|
| Bell ○ | ○ Coinneal |
| Candle ○ | ○ Maróg |
| Christmas tree ○ | ○ Sneachta |
| Christmas card ○ | ○ Réinfhia |
| Pudding ○ | ○ Bronntanais |
| Christmas ○ | ○ Simléar |
| Cracker ○ | ○ Réalta |
| Reindeer ○ | ○ Carr sleamhnáin |
| Snow ○ | ○ Cloigín |
| Stocking ○ | ○ Cárta Nollag |
| Chimney ○ | ○ Stoca |
| Presents ○ | ○ Pléascóg |
| Gloves ○ | ○ Cuileann |
| Sleigh ○ | ○ Crann Nollag |
| Holly ○ | ○ Lámhainn |
| Star ○ | ○ Nollaig |

# RIDDLE ME THIS!

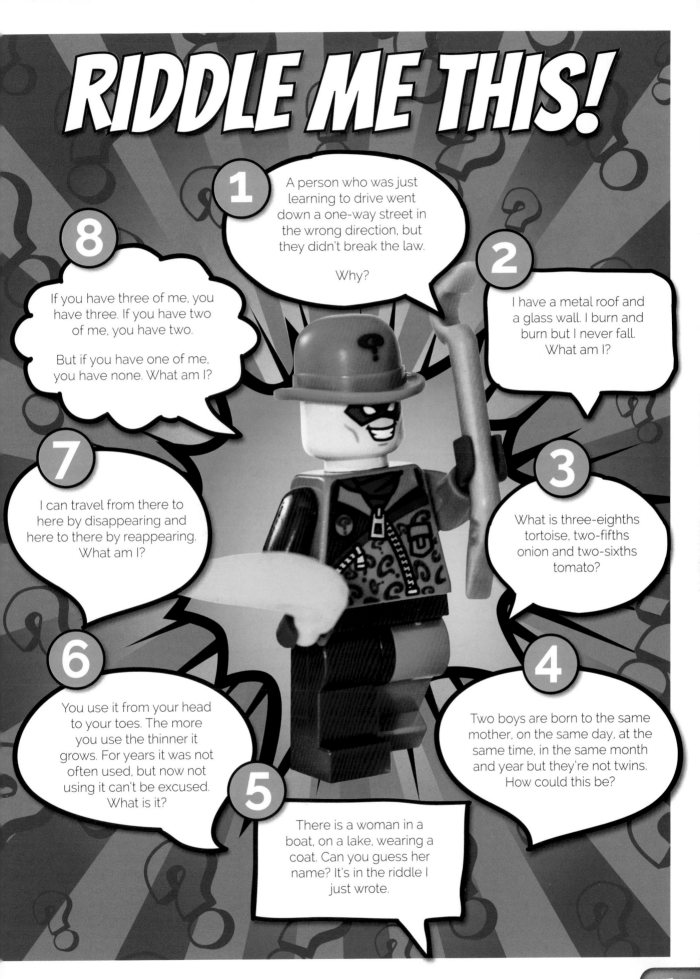

**1** A person who was just learning to drive went down a one-way street in the wrong direction, but they didn't break the law.

Why?

**2** I have a metal roof and a glass wall. I burn and burn but I never fall. What am I?

**3** What is three-eighths tortoise, two-fifths onion and two-sixths tomato?

**4** Two boys are born to the same mother, on the same day, at the same time, in the same month and year but they're not twins. How could this be?

**5** There is a woman in a boat, on a lake, wearing a coat. Can you guess her name? It's in the riddle I just wrote.

**6** You use it from your head to your toes. The more you use the thinner it grows. For years it was not often used, but now not using it can't be excused. What is it?

**7** I can travel from there to here by disappearing and here to there by reappearing. What am I?

**8** If you have three of me, you have three. If you have two of me, you have two.

But if you have one of me, you have none. What am I?

# Memory Game

Look at the picture for 30 seconds and then go to page 28 to see how many questions you can answer from memory!

# Findaword

## WINTER HOLIDAY

Find all these words about having fun outdoors in the winter holidays and cross them off the box of letters. The leftover letters will reveal something cosy to do when you go inside.

| | | | | | | | | | | | | |
|---|---|---|---|---|---|---|---|---|---|---|---|---|
| S | S | S | E | K | A | L | F | W | O | N | S | D |
| N | E | N | C | E | L | Y | T | S | E | E | R | F |
| E | T | O | B | O | G | G | A | N | L | A | W | N |
| T | A | W | H | S | L | E | D | C | O | E | A | A |
| T | K | A | S | S | R | D | I | B | B | M | E | M |
| I | S | N | U | K | W | C | W | O | W | P | W | T |
| M | E | G | U | L | I | O | B | O | I | T | H | A |
| O | C | E | H | O | N | S | N | T | J | T | C | S |
| L | I | L | H | S | L | S | O | S | A | C | O | E |
| A | L | S | C | E | T | I | H | W | C | A | T | P |
| L | E | A | I | C | E | H | O | C | K | E | Y | O |
| S | R | G | N | I | L | R | U | C | E | D | R | L |
| F | H | I | G | L | O | V | E | S | T | N | K | S |

BOBSLEIGH
BOOTS
COLD
CURLING
FREE STYLE
GLOVES
ICE HOCKEY
ICE SKATES
ICICLES

JACKET
LUGE
MITTENS
SCARF
SKIS
SLALOM
SLED
SLEET
SLOPES

SNOW ANGELS
SNOW-BOARD
SNOW-FLAKES
SNOWMAN
SNOWSHOES
TOBOGGAN
WHITE

MYSTERY ANSWER:

# Spellbound

## ACROSS

1. The pretty flower of a fruit tree
5. Largest mammal, ... whale
6. A dull thump
8. These creatures swim in the sea
1. What you have to do at a red light
3. Opposite of asleep
4. A juicy purple stone fruit
6. A sound that bounces back at you
8. A clever thought, a bright ...
0. The part a dog wags
1. Cooking instructions

## DOWN

1. Male cattle or elephants
2. Ten minus nine equals this
3. Be seated in a chair
4. World's highest peak, ... Everest
7. Huge fairy tale man
9. Another word for unwell or sick
10. Type of sandwich meat
11. You use your eyes to do this
12. ... & aah
15. Below or beneath
17. Pieces of metal money
19. The shape of a rainbow
20. Spinning toy

# Interview with Sarah Webb

Sarah Webb is an award-winning children's writer from Dublin. She has written several popular books for children, including *A Sailor Went to Sea, Sea, Sea,* which is a collection of poems and rhymes, and the *Ask Amy Green* series. In 2015, Sarah was awarded the Children's Books Ireland Award for Outstanding Contribution to Children's Books. Last year, she published a very successful non-fiction book called *Blazing a Trail: Irish Women Who Changed the World.* Her second non-fiction book, *Dare to Dream: Irish People Who Took on the World (and Won!),* came out this year. When she's not writing her own books, Sarah is busy mentoring other aspiring authors. She visits libraries, schools and festivals where she shares her writing insights and gives creative writing workshops. She also reviews children's books for the *Irish Independent* newspaper. If you are interested in writing, read on to find out how Sarah got started and what advice she has to offer.

**Hi Sarah. Thanks for taking the time to answer all our questions!**

**Did you always want to be a writer?**

I've always written stories, poems and short books, ever since I was about 10 or 11. My mum kept a lot of my childhood stories, which is great. One of them is called *The Magic Sofa* and is about brothers and sisters who go on an adventure on a flying sofa – rather like a flying carpet but more comfortable. I was very inspired by Enid Blyton's books and also fairy tales. I was lucky enough to have parents who read to me.

My grandfather was an academic writer and a poet and our family really respected and loved books and stories. So I always wanted to tell my own stories – I think a lot of big readers do. But I never dreamed they would actually be published one day!

**Who were your favourite authors as a child?**

When I was very young I adored *Busy, Busy World* by an American writer and illustrator called Richard Scarry.

I loved picture-books; I still do. I also loved Dr. Seuss and when I was able to read confidently by myself (which didn't happen until I was 9) I loved *The Lion, The Witch and the Wardrobe* by Belfast writer C.S. Lewis, and also the books of Judy Blume, who writes about friendship and family issues in a very honest and interesting way. If you like Jacqueline Wilson, you'll like Judy's books!

I also read Irish writers such as Patricia Lynch, Walter Macken and Eilís Dillon, who wrote brilliant adventure novels for children which were set in Ireland.

There are lots of books set in Ireland now, but when I was a girl there were very few, so when I found one I was thrilled. There is something very special about seeing your own country on the pages of a book.

**Your first children's book, *Kids Can Cook* was published in 1997. Why did you decide to write this book?**

I was working in Waterstone's as a children's bookseller in 1997 and customers often asked me for a cookery book for children with Irish recipes in it. There wasn't one on the market so I thought that maybe I could write one – even though I'm not the world's best cook! I needed to try and earn some extra money too as I was a single mum at the time, bringing up my young son on my own. I really wanted to try and buy an old second-hand car to get him to his childminder's house in the morning while I went to work, and back home again when I collected him after work. So I wrote up a proposal for *Kids Can Cook* and sent it out to seven different Irish publishers. Most of the publishers said no – but one, Rena Dardis from The Children's Press, took a chance on me and the book went on to sell very well. It paid for a small silver Honda which cost £500! I'll always be grateful to Rena for giving me my first start (and my first car!).

**You worked as a children's bookseller for many years. Could you tell us a little bit about this job?**

I loved being a children's bookseller. I worked in several different bookshops, from Hodges Figgis, to Hughes & Hughes, Waterstone's and Eason. I would select the new titles to stock in the shop, organise the displays, tidy the shelves (hard work if it had been busy: the picture-books were always in a right state after the weekend), recommend books to customers and arrange writer talks for schools and families. That was one of my favourite parts of the job. One of the first writer events I organised in the shop was with Marita Conlon-McKenna. She sent me a lovely letter after the event to say thank you. I am delighted to say we are now close friends!

**The _Ask Amy Green_ series was your first fictional children's book. Where did you come up with the idea for the character of Amy? Did you always plan on writing a whole series about her?**

Amy was based on me as a 13-year-old girl growing up in Dublin. From the start, I planned it as a series of six books. Amy goes from being quite nervous in book one and relying on her aunt, Clover (who is only 17) a lot, to really coming into her own in book six and standing on her own two feet. I loved writing the Amy Green books!

**How is writing fiction different from writing real-life stories?**

It's very different: you are building a whole world – the setting (unless it is based on a real place, of course), creating characters and inventing dialogue. It's a far more immersive experience. But I also like making real people come to life on the page – that's a different skill. And I love the research that goes into both forms of writing – fiction and non-fiction.

**Do you have a daily ritual when it comes to writing?**

I write in the mornings on Monday, Tuesday and Wednesday. I do some yoga, walk the dog and then sit down at my desk. It's at a window so it's nice and bright. But when I'm writing, I get lost in my own world so I don't notice what is happening outside. I also turn off my phone and the internet so I don't get distracted – that's important! I like to work alone and in a quiet space, the only person who is allowed in the room while I'm writing is the dog.

**Your latest book _Dare to Dream: Irish People Who Took on the World (and Won!)_ is about remarkable Irish people who have changed the world. Could you tell us about this book and why you decided to write it?**

While I was writing _Blazing a Trail: Irish Women Who Changed the World_, I came across so many remarkable Irish women. Because of space restrictions, I had to leave some of them out, so it's great to be able to write about them in a new book. I also wanted to add some of my favourite male heroes – from Tom Crean to Bob Geldof, who grew up near where I live in Dún Laoghaire. He raised millions for famine relief in Africa with Band Aid and Live Aid and is also a successful musician in his own right.

The book tells the stories of 'dreamers' from all over Ireland – scientists, sports people, actors, activists, artists – all kinds of different people. From Cora Staunton, who is a brilliant GAA player; to Ronnie Delany, who was one of the first people in the world to run a sub-four-minute mile; it's been fascinating to research.

The illustrations in the book are by a young Irish artist called Graham Corcoran and he's really captured the spirit of the different people.

**How did you research the Irish people that you wrote about in _Dare to Dream_?**

I researched each person carefully – using books, podcasts, documentaries, newspaper articles and interviews. I also asked some experts in the different fields for name suggestions and advice. When you are writing about real people it's vital to get all the facts right.

I couldn't have written the book without the help of my local library, the Lexicon in Dún Laoghaire. I ordered many of my research books from there and they are always so kind and helpful when I need to find something.

**You run creative writing workshops and visit schools and libraries. Do you think this is an important thing to do?**

Yes, I think being creative is really important. It's how we express ourselves. Some people express themselves through dance, others paint or sing, some garden or cook, or even show who they are through how they dress. I express myself through my writing.

I run five writing clubs at the moment (soon to be six!) for children and teenagers. I love guiding young writers, helping them find their own way of expressing themselves, their own writing 'voice'. I'm delighted to say that some of the club members have even won national writing competitions. They are such a talented bunch!

**What do you enjoy most about being a writer? What do you enjoy least?**

I love when the writing is going well and I'm lost in my story – that's a real joy. The hardest thing about being a writer is finding time to actually write. There isn't anything about the writing process that I dislike, to be honest. I like it all, especially the fun of creating something new. The half-way point when you are writing a book, knowing you have a lot more writing to do, that can be hard, but you just have to push through and keep going.

### What advice would you give to any aspiring writer who is reading this interview?

I'd tell young writers to keep writing, to write as often as possible and to try lots of different genres and forms. Try poetry. And it's important to know that poetry doesn't have to rhyme – look at a wide range of poetry in books or online and see what kind of poetry you like. Try short stories. Try romance, horror, historical fiction. Have fun playing on the page.

Also read widely – again lots of different forms and genres.

And finally, try to finish your work. Don't abandon the story you are writing for a glittering new idea that pops into your head. Jot down the idea and go back to what you're working on.

Above all, don't give up. Keep writing!

### Do you have any favourite writing exercises you'd like to share?

Today my writing clubs will be writing to music. I've chosen some movie soundtracks and I'll be playing them different instrumental pieces and they will write a poem or short story inspired by the music.

Try picking music that evokes or stirs lots of different moods – sad, happy, thoughtful, etc.

I also keep a folder full of pictures of people with interesting faces. There's a magazine called *National Geographic* which is particularly good for photographs from around the world. I give each young writer a photo and ask them to create a story about the person in the photo.

### What books have you read recently that you would recommend to our readers?

I mostly read children's books and I especially like picture books and comic books (sometimes called graphic novels). Some people think that picture books are for young children but the ones that I most enjoy are an intoxicating and thought-provoking blend of art and ideas, like Shaun Tan's *Rules Of Summer* and *The Dam* by David Almond, illustrated by Levi Pinfold. I think my favourite picture book at the moment has to be *Cloth Lullaby: The Woven Life of Louise Bourgeois* by Amy Novesky, illustrated by Isabelle Arsenault. It's the fascinating story of a French-American artist and sculptor, and the illustrations truly sing. I'd highly recommend it if you're looking for something a little different to read!

### And now for some quick-fire questions!

| Question | Answer |
| --- | --- |
| What is your favourite thing about Christmas? | Spending time with my family and friends. And all the sparkling lights and decorations on Christmas trees – it really is a magical time of the year. |
| What is the best Christmas present you got as a child? | A Sindy doll of my very own – she had blonde hair and big blue eyes and I played with her for years. I still have her, in fact. |
| If you could meet anyone in the world, dead or alive, who would it be? | I would like to meet Dr James Barry – who was actually a Cork woman called Margaret Bulkley. She was a surgeon in the nineteenth century and I researched her while writing *Blazing a Trail*. |
| Who or what inspires you? | People from history who overcame great obstacles to do great things. And nature and animals really inspire me too. And finally, children – I run writing clubs for young writers and they are so good at coming up with ideas. |
| If you had to pick a different career, what would it be? | I'd happily be a children's bookseller again. Or a marine biologist, as I'm fascinated by whales. |
| Name one place in the world, apart from Ireland, you would like to live. | Iceland – it's a remarkable place, full of mystery and extremes. We did a road trip around the island last year and I loved it. |
| Who is your favourite singer or band? | An American musician called Tom Waits who tells the most startling, arresting and moving stories in his songs. I also enjoy singing along to Abba in the kitchen – it makes me happy. |
| What is your favourite book? | *Where the Wild Things Are* by Maurice Sendak. |
| What is your favourite film? | *Field of Dreams* with Kevin Costner – it's an old film about baseball and stories and following your dreams. I also love *Jerry Maguire*. For some strange reason, I've always been drawn to sports films – I think it's because they are often about underdogs. |
| Finally, do you remember getting *Sonas* when you were in primary school? | No, sadly not – I wish I had – as I love annuals! |

# Book Quiz

1. What is the name of the detective agency in the *Murder Most Unladylike* series by Robin Stevens?

2. Which First World War novel by Michael Morpurgo has also been made into a film and a stage musical?

   war horse

3. Tom, Amber and Robin are all characters in which book by David Walliams?

4. What is the real name of author and YouTuber Zoella?

   zoe

5. What is the second book in the *Knights of the Borrowed Dark* series by Dave Rudden?

6. In the *Artemis Fowl* series by Eoin Colfer, what type of creature is Holly Short?

7. In the *Harry Potter* books, how does a game of Quidditch end?

8. *Sapphire Battersea* is the sequel to which book by Jacqueline Wilson?

9. What school do Pat and Isabel O'Sullivan go to in the books by Enid Blyton?

10. In *Little Women*, what is the name of the youngest of the four sisters?

11. Which classic children's book features the Cheshire Cat, the Mad Hatter and the March Hare?

12. In the children's books by Emma Donoghue, what is the name of the large family of which Sumac is a member?

13. *Five Children on the Western Front* by Kate Saunders is a sequel to which children's classic by E. Nesbit?

14. What is the name of the skeleton detective created by Derek Landy?

15. *Turtles All the Way Down* and *Looking for Alaska* were written by which American author?

16. Who is the author of *Divergent*?

17. What is the name of the lion in *The Lion, the Witch and the Wardrobe*?

18. *Game Changer* is the autobiography of which Mayo Gaelic football star?

19. In *The Hunger Games*, who is the other tribute from District 12 along with Katniss?

20. Auggie, Jack and Summer are characters in which book by R.J. Palacio?

# Letter Scramble

Cross off the letters that appear more than once and then rearrange the letters left to spell out the mystery answers.

## 1

MYSTERY ANSWER:

G A S D O C H E O P P A Q U M F R K D S K W A D M G U G W A Q K U I P C N B

## 2

MYSTERY ANSWER:

B M V L T G A Q C F D O W J E W S C V H G Q P M F P I V M W D N H O B J A G D

24

# Tarraing & Dathaigh

Dathaigh an pictiúr iomlán – úsáid an ghreille.

# Swimming in a Sea of Plastic

## Ten Things You Should Know

**SAY NO TO SINGLE-USE PLASTIC**

**1** More than 300 million tonnes of plastic is produced globally every year. *Remember: 1 tonne = 1,000 kg.* That is a lot of plastic and half of it is only used once before it is thrown away. That type of plastic is called 'single-use plastic' and includes things like drinking straws, disposable cutlery and plastic bags. Did you know that a plastic bag has an average 'working life' of only 15 minutes?

**2** The demand for plastic has increased dramatically over the last 70 years. In the last 10 years alone, we have produced more plastic than in the whole of the last century. Astoundingly, one million plastic bottles are bought around the world every minute, and this number is set to rise by another 20 per cent by 2021 – if we don't change our ways.

**3** Only about 9 per cent of plastic in the world has been recycled: 12 per cent has been incinerated, polluting the air with toxic gases as it burns, and the remaining 79 per cent remains in the environment. That plastic is here to stay – nearly every piece of plastic ever made still exists today because there is no organism that can break it down completely.

**4** At least 8 million tonnes of plastic enter the oceans each year. That's like emptying a rubbish truck of plastic into an ocean every single minute! Almost 80 per cent of that plastic comes from the land (e.g. from rivers and littered beaches) while 20 per cent comes from ships at sea, including from fishing.

**5** There are five massive 'garbage patches' of plastic, also known as gyres, in the oceans around the world. These huge collections of plastic debris cover large swaths of the ocean. The largest one, located between California and Hawaii and known as the Great Pacific Garbage Patch, is three times the size of France.

**6** Sadly, animals pay a heavy price for our plastic waste. Ocean plastic kills millions of marine animals every year. Nearly 700 species, including endangered ones, are known to have been affected by it. Some are visibly harmed —caught up in abandoned fishing nets or discarded six-pack rings. While others suffer internal problems: they mistakenly eat plastic that blocks their digestive systems, and they die later from starvation.

# Garbage Patches Map

80% of the waste enters the ocean from the shore.

North Atlantic gyre

Great Pacific Garbage Patch
**1,760,000 km²**

South Pacific gyre

South Atlantic gyre

Indian Ocean gyre

20% of the waste is emitted from ships.

## 7

The United Nations (UN) has warned of the growing threat of plastic pollution to human health. Many of the fish we eat have, at one time or another, ingested small pieces of plastic called microplastics. All over the world, scientists are researching what this means for human health.

PLASTIC WASTE
BREAK DOWN
MICROPLASTIC
?
MISTAKE FOR FOOD
ENTER FOOD CHAIN

## 9

Governments also need to take action to help clean up the oceans. By introducing bans or taxes on plastic products, people can change their behaviour and cut down on the amount of plastic thrown away. In 2002 Ireland became the first country in the world to impose a plastic bag tax, which helped to greatly reduce plastic waste. Some countries have gone a step further and banned plastic bags altogether. Since 2017, anyone in Kenya who is found using, producing or selling a plastic bag faces up to four years in jail or a hefty fine.

## 8

Thankfully, there are solutions to the ocean plastic crisis – but they require us to change our lifestyles. One of the easiest ways you can help is by reducing single-use plastics. Avoid single-use plastics that you do not need (e.g. straws, plastic bags, takeaway containers). You can also use reusable products such as flasks and bags for life.

## 10

Technology is helping to clean up our oceans. The Ocean Cleanup is an environmental non-governmental organisation (NGO) based in the Netherlands. They have developed special barriers that are placed in ocean garbage patches that are designed to scoop up debris. They predict their project could clean up 50 per cent of the debris in the Great Pacific Garbage Patch within five years.

# Broken Hearted

Mend these broken hearts to form the names of ten couples who carved their names on a tree, only to find it chopped down and split in half. There's only one way to get all ten couples together correctly.

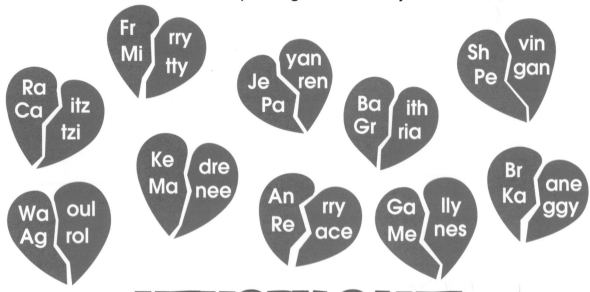

## MEMORY GAME QUESTIONS

**For page 18**

**1.** Is Santa in the picture?

NO!

**2.** How many pinecones are there?

four

**3.** What colour is the candle?

red

**4.** Are there any stars in the picture?

**5.** How many snowmen are there?

**6.** What winter footwear is hanging by some string?

**7.** Is there a Christmas tree decoration?

**8.** What colour jewels make up the stripe on the present?

# READERS' JOKES!

**Q: What do elves learn in school?**

A: The elfabet!

Caoimhe McKeogh, St Mary's National School, Raharney, Co. Westmeath

**Q: What happened when the boy put his wooden shoes in the toilet?**

A: It got clogged!

Caoimhe Ahern, Gealscoil Donnacha Rua, Co. Clare

**Q: What do you call a deer with no eyes?**
A: No idear!

**Q: What do you call a deer with no eyes and no legs?**
A: Still no idear!

Hannah Lucey, Vicarstown National School, Co. Cork

**Q: What is red, white and blue at Christmas?**

A: A sad candy cane!

Dayna Duffy, St Mary's National School, Raharney, Co. Westmeath

**Q: Why was the turkey not hungry?**

A: Because he was stuffed!

Anna Johnston, St Mary's National School, Raharney, Co. Westmeath

**Q: How do angels greet each other?**

A: Halo!

**Q: Where do Christmas plants go when they want to be movie stars?**
A: Holly-wood!

Alex Peters, Castletara National School, Co. Cavan

# FUN FACT!

The world's largest gift was the Statue of Liberty. It was gifted by France to the USA in 1886. It is over 93 m high and weighs 225 tonnes.

Folens Fun Fact!

# TONGUE-TWISTER!

How many cookies could a good cook cook, if a good cook could cook cookies? A good cook could cook as many cookies as a good cook who could cook cookies.

Folens Tongue-Twister Challenge!

**Thank you to all the *Sonas* readers who sent in great jokes!**

# BEES

Did you know that without bees many of our fruit and vegetables could not grow, and wildflowers across Ireland would begin to disappear?

## Just the facts, pleazzzze!

There are 97 different species of bees in Ireland. The ones most familiar to us are honeybees and bumblebees. Honeybees live in hives, where they make enough honey for themselves and for us to eat! Bumblebees are easily recognisable because of their chubby, furry, striped bodies. Even though some bees have stingers, there's no reason for us to fear them. Bees won't attack unless they feel threatened. In fact, bees are much more helpful than you might think.

## Pollination: What's the buzz?

Flowers use pollen to make seeds from which new plants can grow. To make a seed, the pollen from one flower needs to be moved to a nearby flower of the same type – this is called pollination. Flowers can't move pollen by themselves. This is where bees come in. Bees eat nectar, which is found in flowers. When a bee lands on a flower, pollen sticks to the hairs on the bee's body. The bee collects the pollen into a ball to carry home for hungry baby bees to eat. As the bee moves from flower to flower, it drops and collects more pollen. In other words, it pollinates. Without pollination, plants wouldn't be able to produce the fruit and seeds that many animals and birds rely on for food. But that's not all. Bees also pollinate many of the delicious fruits and vegetables we love to eat – strawberries, apples, pears, beans and blackberries! If it weren't for bees, these flowers and plants would struggle to grow, and some would disappear completely!

*Fun fact: A strawberry flower needs five visits from a bumblebee or 15 visits from a honeybee before it can turn into a strawberry!*

## Dangerzzzz facing bees

Bees are in danger of becoming extinct. They face lots of threats, including habitat loss and exposure to harmful chemicals used on crops. Drastic changes in weather and climate have added to the decline in the bee population. It's vital that humans take action to protect bees and allow them to continue their important work.

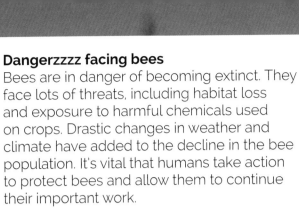

### Helpful ideazzzz

Plant flowers in your school so that bees will have food from spring to autumn.

Plant a shrub, like willow or hazel. These flower in spring and provide food for bees.

Bees love weeds such as dandelions. If you have lots of long grass around your school, ask if a small portion of weeds can be kept for the bees.

Visit www.pollinators.ie and download the *Junior All-Ireland Pollinator Plan 2015–2020*. It's packed full of information and practical ideas about how you can get behind bees and give them the buzz they need to keep on pollinating!

# Art & Craft

## What to do:

Preparation: Before you begin, gather the materials for the cracker contents. Write some jokes on the paper squares. If you want to make your own paper crowns, follow the steps on page 33.

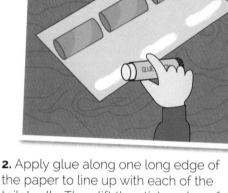

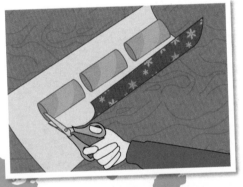

**1.** Measure the wrapping paper you will need by lining up three toilet roll tubes along the paper, as shown. Cut off any excess paper to the side. Then cut along the edge, making sure there's enough paper to wrap around the rolls completely.

**2.** Apply glue along one long edge of the paper to line up with each of the toilet rolls. Then lift the sticky edge of the paper up and over the rolls, gluing this sticky edge to the opposite (unglued) edge. There will be no glue on the toilet rolls, and they will sit securely in the wrapping paper.

**3.** Optional: If you are using a cracker snap, ask an adult to help you apply a little glue to both ends and place it carefully inside the cracker.

**4.** Slightly pull the end toilet roll away from the middle toilet roll to create a tiny gap between them. Push them back together to make a crease. Then gently twist the end around. Wrap a piece of ribbon around the twisted part and tie it in a bow.

# Christmas Crackers

## What you need:

### For crackers
- Festive wrapping paper
- Toilet roll tubes (3 per cracker)
- Cracker snaps (optional)
- Festive ribbon or string
- Scissors
- Glue stick

### For cracker contents
- White paper, cut into small squares (for jokes)
- A pen or marker
- Wrapped chocolates, e.g. Heroes, Celebrations or Roses
- Small toys or trinkets, e.g. golf tees, pencil toppers, marbles
- Paper crowns (to make your own, follow the instructions below)
- Confetti (optional)

**5.** Carefully pull the toilet roll out from the end. If you put in a cracker snap, find where it is and gently press the glued part to the paper so that it stays in place.

**6.** Place a joke, a paper crown, some treats and confetti into the open end of the cracker. Give it a shake so that they fall into the centre. Then repeat Steps 4 and 5 at the other end of the cracker.

## To make paper crowns

**1.** Cut a strip of craft tissue paper 10–12 cm wide, and long enough to wrap around your head.

**2.** Fold the paper in half and glue the ends together.

**3.** Fold the paper three or four times until it is about 5 cm long.

**4.** Cut an angled line along the top edge of the crown, as shown.

**5.** Unfold the crown and try it on! Then fold it back up so that it will fit inside the Christmas cracker.

# Aimsigh na Focail

Aimsigh na focail seo sa ghreille.

**DEARG**
RED

**AINGEAL**
ANGEL

**CLOIGÍN**
BELL

**NOLLAIG**
CHRISTMAS

**SÍOFRA**
ELF

**MÁLA**
BAG

**SNEACHTA**
SNOW

**LITIR**
LETTER

**GRÁ**
LOVE

**FÉASÓG**
BEARD

**CRANN**
TREE

| G | Ó | S | A | É | F | O | W | S | A | S | F | L | V |
|---|---|---|---|---|---|---|---|---|---|---|---|---|---|
| U | L | J | X | W | N | R | Y | P | T | I | L | C | S |
| E | A | N | S | N | I | H | X | K | H | O | Á | T | U |
| B | C | Q | E | T | D | M | U | K | C | C | C | U | U |
| V | C | K | I | P | W | K | T | Q | A | F | R | A | V |
| R | P | L | É | A | S | C | Ó | G | E | M | J | C | S |
| G | É | G | K | C | C | X | S | F | N | Q | L | T | C |
| Ó | I | I | M | M | R | Í | T | R | S | A | Á | V | L |
| R | F | A | N | N | O | T | K | T | E | B | O | U | O |
| A | A | Q | L | F | N | Á | R | G | L | X | C | P | I |
| M | Y | L | R | L | H | A | N | A | D | E | A | R | G |
| V | D | A | Á | O | O | I | R | H | E | C | Y | P | Í |
| S | N | X | T | M | A | N | A | C | K | S | N | P | N |
| E | I | Q | L | A | E | N | N | I | O | C | T | W | E |

**MARÓG**
PUDDING

**CÁCA**
CAKE

**COINNEAL**
CANDLE

**PLÉASCÓG**
CRACKER

**RÉINFHIA**
REINDEER

**SIOC**
FROST

**STOCA**
STOCKING

**STÁBLA**
STABLE

34

# Hexoku

Fit the numbers 1–6 into each hexagon so that where
the hexagons touch, the numbers are the same.
No number can be repeated in any hexagon.

# Mixed Messages

y Oliver Schuch, Paddock National School, Co. Laois
irst Place – 2018 *Sonas* Creative Writing Competition

'What on Earth is that?' muttered Zorge to himself, staring through his intergalactic binoculars. 'Could it be a glowing multicoloured meteorite?' he wondered, sitting in his pilot chair in the command module aboard his space ship. 'Or maybe it's a Cosmic Ray ...'

He logged on to his onboard computer and searched for images but nothing similar showed up on the search results. Travelling through space, he was aware of what eclipses and comets and electromagnetic waves looked like in the distance. But this was different. He decided to check his GPS coordinates instead and, according to the Spacemap, the strange glowing seemed to be indeed coming from the planet Earth. At first, he thought it was an object moving towards the planet but, as he got closer to the Earth's magnetosphere, he could see it was actually coming from the Earth's surface.

As he entered the magnetosphere, his spacecraft started to wobble and his computer started to experience a strange interference. He engaged the reaction control system to stabilise the spacecraft and then consulted his electromagnetic radio to decipher what was causing the interference. One single message was being repeated over and over but what it meant was unknown to him. The interference was coming from Earth's satellites in orbit around the planet. One single message jamming the entire network!

HAPPY_NEW_YEAR.

This foreign communication meant nothing to Zorge. Was it some type of SOS signal or an ABORT message? He steered his spaceship as close as he dared to the flashing visual signals coming from Earth's surface. There were small UFOs (Unidentified Flashing Objects) outlining pathways, streets, buildings and hundreds of earthlings were all gathered together in a massive assembly. Other sounds were now coming through on his electromagnetic radio. The earthlings appeared to be chanting in unison, looking towards the night sky. The sound coming through the speaker sounded like:

7 ... 6 ... 5 ... 4 ... 3 ... 2 ... 1!!!

Suddenly Zorge was blinded by a bright blast right in front of his command module window. Several of these loud explosions were shot from Earth into the sky, all displaying a bright array of colours. The earthlings below were now cheering happily and appeared to seem victorious. Zorge did not feel welcome to approach Earth and as he swerved to avoid the explosions, he turned on his light-speed turbos and headed back out into deep space. As Zorge's light-speed turbos emitted bright orange and white flames, a small boy on Earth looked up, pointed into the sky and shouted to his Mum: 'WHAT ON EARTH IS THAT?!'

# Christmas Findaword

Find the Christmas words hiding in the box of letters. The words can be found in straight lines up, down, forwards, backwards or even diagonally. The leftover letters will reveal the mystery answer.

ACTIVITY

ANGEL

ANTICIPATION

AROMA

BAUBLES

BEAUTIFUL

BELLS

BERRIES

BISCUITS

BLITZEN

BOOTS

BOXES

BRANCHES

BUSTLING

CANDLES

CANDY CANES

CAROLS

CELEBRATION

CHARITABLE

CHEERFUL

CHESTNUTS

CHILDREN

CHIMING

CHIMNEY

COLD

COMET

CONTENTMENT

DASHER

DECEMBER

DECORATIONS

DELIGHT

DESSERT

DINNER

EVERGREEN

EXCITEMENT

FROLIC

GAMES

GARLAND

GINGERBREAD

GIVING

GREETINGS

GUESTS

HAT

HEARTFELT

HOLIDAY

HOME

HOPEFUL

HOSPITALITY

HOT CHOCOLATE

HUGS

ICICLES

LEISURELY

LETTERS

LIGHTS

LIST

LOLLIES

LOVE

MAIL

MEANINGFUL

MERRY

MITTENS

NICE

NORTH POLE

OCCASION

ORNAMENTS

PACKAGE

PARADE

PARTRIDGE

PLAYING

PLEASANT

PRANCER

RECEIVE

RED NOSE

REINDEER

RELATIVES

RIBBON

RITUAL

SCARF

SEASON

SINGING

THRILL

TOYS

TRADITION

TRIFLE

TRIMMINGS

TWINKLING

WAITING

WINTERTIME

WISH

WONDERMENT

```
S E L D N A C T I V I T Y D D R E B O O T S
S N N E R D L I H C Y C P A C K A G E A M T
D T O L T O Y S O Y E T S L A U T I R T I U
A S H I N G I C P L L H I O B G I V I N G N
E E O G T W C S E E E V O L S D E S S E R T
R X T H I A E B F R N S E R A C M G A M E S
B O C T S L R T U U O S E V I T A L E R M E
R B H I C A R O L S I T G N I T I A W E O H
E N O I T A P I C I T N A S A E L P R D H C
G N C I E E F O S E I L L O L C C R S N A N
N I O H M Y M W L L D U I F A O Y E O O H A
I N L M I E E K B A F I N L N T D R W H R
G E A E T M G N N A R R G D G T R N N Y D B
N E T A R N I D M T T E O I S E I O A A E I
I R E N E W O N I I L E T M C N M S M D C S
S G N I T E E R G R H H E N A T M E E I E C
N R E N N I D C T A T C A C R M I I N L M U
E E Z G I H A L R H R R I T F E N R T O B I
T V T F W I R I S C P L A Y I N G R S H E T
T E I U S E A S O N O O A P S T S E U G R S
I S L L E B P T H R I L L N N O B B I R U T
M M B E A U T I F U L R E E D N I E R A S H
```

MYSTERY ANSWER:

# CRAZY BRAIN FACTS

Your brain is a pretty amazing organ!
It controls everything in your body
and enables you to think, feel
and store memories.
Read on to learn more.

## How does a human brain work?

· There are 100 billion neurons present in the brain.

· Neurons send messages from your brain to your spinal cord which then sends it to other body parts. This message is called an impulse. It happens so fast that you don't even think about doing it. For example, if you touch your finger on something hot, your brain makes you quickly pull your hand away before you get burned.

· The right side of the brain controls the left side of the body, and vice versa.

· The brain is protected by the skull, which is made up of 22 bones fused together.

· The brain is 60 per cent fat, making it one of the fattest organs in the human body.

· The brain is just 2 per cent of your body weight, but uses 20 per cent of all your energy.

## Learning new skills

· Playing chess improves your brain power. It helps you to slow down, concentrate and understand complex patterns.

· Music helps young children's language development.

· The development of the brain from birth to age 3 is the fastest rate of development of our whole lives.

· Reading aloud to children helps stimulate brain development.

· We are more likely to remember something if we make an effort to understand it and if we review it regularly – this helps the connections between neurons in the brain.

## Making memories

- A good night's sleep helps your memory to work better! While you are asleep, your brain moves the new things you learned that day to a more efficient storage part of your brain.

- If you are trying to remember something, close your eyes! Research shows that we can remember up to 23 per cent more without visual distractions.

- Saying something out loud helps us to remember it later. This makes sense when you're learning your tables!

- Of all the five senses, the one most closely linked to memory is our sense of smell. Smells can bring particular moments in time vividly to life.

- Taking a photo of something actually makes us less likely to remember it. The brain focuses on the process of taking the photo, instead of focusing on the thing itself!

- If you know you can access information quickly (e.g. on the internet) you are less likely to remember it.

- Your memory could hold 2.5 petabytes of data – the equivalent of a video that's 300 years long!

## Strange but true!

- The brain processes about 70,000 thoughts every day!

- We forget 90 per cent of our dreams as soon as we wake up.

- Most adults can't remember anything from before the age of 3.

- Compared to other mammals of similar size to us, the human brain is three times larger.

- Evolution has led the human brain to become more complex and able to carry out more functions.

- The famous scientist Albert Einstein wore a grey suit almost every day so that he wouldn't have to waste brain power deciding what to wear. Mark Zuckerberg, the owner of Facebook, does the same thing, he wears a grey T-shirt to work every day!

# Word Games

## Last Word Standing

Use the clues to cross out the words in the boxes. One word will be left over.
This last word standing is the mystery answer.

**Clues:**

- All fruits and vegetables
- All toys
- All baby animals
- All winter clothes
- All words that end in 'K'
- All people who wear uniforms
- All pizza toppings
- All numbers

| | | |
|---|---|---|
| HAM | | CALF |
| SCARF | DOLL | FIVE |
| KITE | ORANGE | PUMPKIN |
| SOLDIERS | COAT | FIFTEEN |
| FOAL | PIGLET | GLOVES |
| SKUNK | CHEESE | BACON |
| SNOWMAN | FIREMEN | DRINK |
| GARDAÍ | MONK | PEACH |
| TWELVE | | KITTEN |

## Chainletters

Can you find the 13-letter word hiding in the chain?
You must use all 13 letters once only and you can move from circle to circle but only where they are connected by lines.

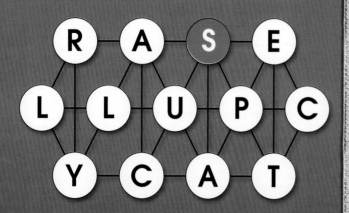

## What's What

Complete the three-letter words, and the middle row across will reveal the solution.

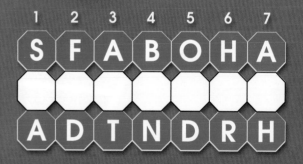

1. Therapeutic bath
2. Short-lived trend
3. Creative work
4. Prohibit
5. Puzzling
6. Opposite of 'him'
7. Mountain tree

# The Sports Quiz

1. Where will the 2020 Olympic Games be held?

2. Which League of Ireland club plays their home games at Tallaght Stadium?

3. In GAA, which county is known as 'the Faithful County'?

4. True or false? Brazil is the only country to have played in every World Cup finals tournament.

5. Ciara Mageean represents Ireland in which sport?

6. Where will the final of Euro 2020 be played?

7. In tennis, what is it called when both players have scored 40 points?

8. In which sport would you find the terms 'albatross', 'birdie' and 'eagle'?

9. How many goals did Robbie Keane score for Ireland?

10. In the USA, the Boston Celtics, LA Lakers and Chicago Bulls play which sport?

11. Olympic medallist Sonia O'Sullivan comes from which county?

12. Which footballer is Belfast Airport named after?

13. In which sport do teams compete for the O'Duffy Cup?

14. Which former Ireland rugby player took part in *Dancing with the Stars* in 2019?

15. What is the surname of brother-and-sister jockeys, Ruby and Katie?

16. In which sport do England and Australia compete for The Ashes?

17. True or false? The triple jump was previously known as the hop, skip and jump.

18. Which American swimmer holds the record number of Olympic medals?

19. What three disciplines are normally found in a triathlon?

20. Which country's rugby team performs the haka before its matches?

STRATEGY

# Maze

Help Emma make her way through the maze, collecting Christmas gifts on the way. When you make it to the other side, count how many of each gift you've collected on the path.

# Aimsigh na Difríochtaí

Aimsigh deich gcinn de dhifríochtaí idir na pictiúir.

# A Shared Secret

by Caoimhe Flannery, Castletownshend National School, Co. Cork
**Second Place – 2018 *Sonas* Creative Writing Competition**

'What on earth is that?' Mia looked across the woodland path to where her friend Ella was pointing. They were in the woods near Mia's house, walking her dog, Dash. Next to the forest map was a stone archway about knee-height. On closer inspection, Mia realised that there was a tunnel behind it, hidden by some bracken.

Suddenly there was a scurry from behind them, as Dash shot past. 'Where's he off to?' Ella wondered aloud.

'He's probably just chasing a rabbit,' Mia replied, peering through the tunnel. She could just see Dash's tail and behind, wedged between the two sides of the tunnel. He was stuck!

Seeing as Ella was the smallest, she squeezed through the tiny archway to try to pull Dash out. With all her strength, Ella managed to free Dash. When she pulled him away, she noticed that the rest of the tunnel was a lot higher. If she bent over, she could surely walk through it.

Ella called Mia to show her what she had discovered. Curiosity got the better of the girls and they decided to see where the souterrain led. The tunnel twisted and turned until suddenly it stopped. In front of them was a circular room. In the centre of it was a pillar with a small box on top.

The girls examined the box. It was padlocked shut but the hinges were coming loose. It looked ancient. Ella picked up the box, turned it over and saw a message engraved on the bottom.

*Solve the puzzle, connect the clues,*
*Then an ancient secret will be known to you.*

Underneath that, the riddle was written.

*IF YOU'VE GOT IT*
*YOU CAN'T SHARE IT,*
*AND IF YOU SHARE IT,*
*YOU HAVEN'T GOT IT.*
*WHAT IS IT?*

Mia hesitated before shouting: 'A secret!'

Suddenly the floor beneath them began to shake. The girls gripped each other in fear. What was happening? The piece of floor they were standing on disappeared down below the ground, taking Mia and Ella with it. The movement came to an abrupt halt and the girls were standing in another room, this one slightly bigger.

In front of them stood another pillar. This one had another inscription:

*This is the last one, so you'll see.*
*Solve the riddle and find the key.*

The girls read the riddle.

*I GET CUT BUT I NEVER BLEED.*
*I HAVE TEETH BUT I DON'T BITE.*
*I GET PUT ON A RING BUT I'M NOT A DIAMOND.*
*I GET TURNED BUT I'M NOT A PAGE.*
*WHAT AM I?*

Ella thought for a moment. 'A key?'

There was a rumble and the pillar fell to the ground, revealing a gold leather notebook hiding beneath it. Mia picked it up and started to leaf through the pages. It was a diary of an 11-year-old girl called Tara who lived during the nineteenth century. Despite being hidden for two hundred years, it was in pristine condition.

The girls were shocked at their revelation … The girl was related to one of them! They knew if they divulged the secret of what lay within the pages, there would be serious consequences. So they promised each other they never would … After all, it was a secret!

# Writing Time

Do you love to write stories? Have you always dreamed of seeing your story in print? Then why not enter the *Sonas* short story competition? You could see your story published in next year's *Sonas*!

**The story must begin with these words:**
**'Everything was going wrong.'**

**See below for all the details you need to enter.**
**Here are some writing tips to help you get started!**

## Inspiration

You can find inspiration for stories in all sorts of different places! Below are just a few.

- Something that happened to you: Did you win a match or get a fantastic present? Did you fall out of a tree, or have a row with your sibling? Good and bad events can get your imagination working!
- Somewhere you visited: How about a place you went on holidays or a trip you took with your family? Or maybe a visit to a museum got you thinking about what it would have been like to live long ago?
- Something you read or saw: Maybe you read something interesting in a book or saw something inspiring on TV or on YouTube?
- A conversation you overheard.

## Getting started

Think about where and when your story will be set – your own neighbourhood or school, Ireland long ago, a galaxy far, far away, or an imaginary world … Let your imagination go wild!

## Characters

Who will be your main character, and what will they be like? Who else will be in your story: their family, friends – or enemies? How will you show the different personalities of your characters?

## Plot

Plan the structure of your story. It needs to have a beginning, middle and end. The most important bit is the problem or conflict your main character has to deal with. How will you introduce this, and how will it all turn out? Think about the climax of the story – where the most exciting thing happens, and the issue is resolved. It doesn't matter if you don't have everything figured out – just start writing and see where your imagination takes you!

## And finally …

Once you've got your first draft finished, it's time to go over it again to make sure it's as good as you can make it! Stories are rarely perfect first time around, so writing another draft will make all the difference. Is there any way you could make your story better? Is everything clear to your reader? Check for spelling and grammar mistakes. Then write it out neatly or type it up.

Good luck and – most important – have fun writing!

# SHORT STORY COMPETITION

**WIN! €100 GIFT CARD!**

Gift Card

SMYTHS

Write a short story (between 300 and 600 words) beginning with these words: 'Everything was going wrong.'

**Please email your story to sonas@folens.ie with the subject line 'Sonas Short Story Competition', or post to:**

*Sonas Short Story Competition*
*Folens Publishers*
*Hibernian Industrial Estate*
*Greenhills Road*
*Tallaght*
*Dublin 24*

The closing date for all entries is 10 January 2020.

The two best stories, as judged by a panel of authors, will be published in next year's annual. The winner will receive a €100 Smyths gift card and the runner-up will receive a €50 Smyths gift card!

By entering this competition you agree that your story can be published by Folens in *Sonas* 2020. Stories will be edited before publication.

# Make It!

## Festive White Chocolate and Raspberry Cheesecake

**Ask an adult to help you make this delicious Christmas cheesecake.
You will need a loose-bottomed cake tin (20 cm).**

### Ingredients:

- 150 g Digestive biscuits
- 50 g butter
- 400 g white chocolate, divided
- 600 g cream cheese, at room temperature
- 50 g caster sugar
- 250 ml double cream
- 250 g raspberries (plus extra to decorate – optional)
- Raspberry coulis or sauce

**1** Put the biscuits in a ziplock bag and use a rolling pin to break them into crumbs. Place the crumbs in a small bowl. Melt the butter and combine it with the biscuit crumbs. Press the biscuit mixture into the base of a loose-bottomed cake tin and leave to cool in the fridge.

**2** Break 300 g of the white chocolate into pieces and gently melt them in a bowl in the microwave. (Leave 100 g of chocolate aside to decorate.)

**3** Beat the cream cheese and sugar together. Lightly whip the double cream, then fold it into the cream cheese mixture. Stir in the melted chocolate.

**4** Add the raspberries to the mixture, then spoon it into the cake tin.

**Tip:** Carefully smooth the top of the cake, especially around the edges, to ensure the cake looks neat when the tin is removed.

**5** Place the cake in the fridge for at least 4 hours, until set.

4 hours

**6** Carefully remove the cheesecake from the tin. Before serving, grate the remaining white chocolate over the top and drizzle with raspberry sauce or coulis. You could also add fresh raspberries.

49

# Interview with
# Dinny Corcoran

Dinny Corcoran grew up in Donabate, north Co. Dublin, and played Gaelic football and soccer, appearing for the famous Dublin schoolboy soccer club Belvedere. He played for the Ireland youth team alongside teammates such as Harry Arter.

When he was still a teenager, Dinny moved to the League of Ireland, starting out with St Patrick's Athletic. Over 12 seasons as a first-team player, he appeared for seven League of Ireland teams: Sporting Fingal, Shelbourne, Drogheda United, Bohemians, St Patrick's Athletic, UCD and Sligo Rovers. He now plays for Bohemians and this is his third spell with the Dublin club.

**Hi Dinny. Thanks for taking the time to answer all our questions!**

**Were you always interested in soccer and what does the sport mean to you?**

When it comes to hobbies, soccer is definitely my main interest. I first joined a soccer team at seven years of age and I've been playing ever since. I'm also a big fan of the Premiership and I watch soccer every weekend. Soccer means a lot to me; it's been my job for the past 12 years and I love it. I don't know what I'd do without soccer.

**What were you like in school? Did you enjoy it?**

I really enjoyed school. I had a lot of good friends and we had great fun. I got on very well with the teachers, so that helped a lot. I wish I could go back to school!

**As well as playing soccer, you used to play Gaelic football. How did you manage to balance the two sports? Is it true that you could have played for Dublin?**

As well as playing soccer, I used to play GAA for my local club, St Patrick's Donabate. It was very tough to balance them both; sometimes I'd have soccer training and GAA training on the same night, so I'd have to miss one. And on the weekends, I'd play a soccer match on a Friday night and then play a GAA match on a Saturday. It was very tiring. As I got older, it was too hard to commit to both sports and I had to make a choice, so I chose soccer as I've always preferred it! When I was playing GAA, I did get a phone call to go and play a cup match for Dublin – but I couldn't, as I had only come back from a serious injury and I wasn't fully fit. If I had chosen GAA instead of soccer, maybe I would have gone on to play for Dublin – but I guess we'll never know!

Republic of Ireland U16 squad; Dinny is third from the left in the top row

**Did you have any heroes (sporting or otherwise) growing up?**

My hero growing up was Damien Duff. He was a great player for the Republic of Ireland and then he joined my favourite football club, Chelsea, so I really liked him and enjoyed watching him play. And luckily enough, I actually got to play against him when he joined Shamrock Rovers towards the end of his career, so that was amazing!

**Some of the best players in the world, including Pelé and Zidane, have played in Dalymount. What's it like to play there every week?**

Playing in Dalymount Park every week is amazing. The fans are brilliant and the atmosphere is always fantastic. It is something I will really miss when I have to retire. It is my favourite stadium in the whole country.

**Can you tell us what a typical day is like for you?**

A typical day for me is waking up around 6:30 a.m. as I have a two-year-old son who gets me up at that time! Then I get my son dressed and make breakfast for both of us at 7 a.m. Then I just relax and play around with my son: most days I bring him to the beach or the park or the play centre! Then we both have lunch and watch some cartoons for the afternoon. At 5 p.m. I leave my house to go training – we start at 6 p.m. After training, I go home and have dinner and watch a movie with my girlfriend – or watch a football match, if I'm lucky! Then around 9:30 p.m. I go to bed.

**You played for the Republic of Ireland at underage level. What are your memories of that?**

I have great memories of playing for the Republic of Ireland at Under-15, Under-16, Under-18 and Under-19 levels. As a young kid, it was always a dream of mine to represent my country. Wearing the green jersey for the first time was something I'll never forget. On my debut, we beat Northern Ireland 4-0 and I managed to score the first goal, so it was an amazing experience. I played with some really good players for Ireland and enjoyed every minute of it.

**Did you or any of your friends have trials with English clubs when you were younger?**

When I was 16 I had trials with Plymouth Argyle Football Club. At the time, they were in the Championship and doing well. After a two-week trial, they offered me a contract but I didn't accept it as I wasn't happy with the contract offer and I wanted to complete my Leaving Cert first. I was also supposed to go on a trial with Cardiff City Football Club but unfortunately that never happened as the club ran into financial difficulties.

**Who is the most famous player you have played against?**

We played against the Ireland senior team in a friendly which included the likes of Robbie Keane, Damien Duff and John O'Shea, so that was a great experience! Another famous player I played against was Gabriel Obertan. He was playing for France Under-19s at the time. Soon after that match, he went on to sign for Manchester United for millions of pounds! He was brilliant when I played against him.

**Outside the football arena, you made the headlines earlier this year by appearing on the Channel 4 show *Countdown*! How did that come about and what was the experience like?**

My mam is a big fan of *Countdown* and, when I was younger, I'd always watch it with her. She thought I was very good at it and always said I should go on it. She then applied for the show on my behalf. I then had to do an exam over the phone, which I passed. That was enough to get me on the show – I couldn't believe it! It was a great experience; I enjoyed it a lot. Unfortunately, when I was on the show, nerves got the better of me and I lost! I'd love to go on again at some stage!

Cumann na mBunscoil, Croke Park; Dinny is first from the right in the front row

**What do you eat to stay fit and healthy? Are you allowed to have occasional treats like takeaways?**

It's very important that I eat good foods in order to stay fit and get the best performance out of myself. My breakfast is usually porridge or Weetabix! For lunch, I'd usually have eggs, beans or turkey breast. And my dinners usually consist of chicken with pasta or rice. I also try to eat a lot of fruit and vegetables throughout each day. And it's important to drink lots of water to stay hydrated. Once a week, every Sunday, I go to my mam's house and treat myself to a takeaway! Other than that, I eat pretty well!

**Why do you think sport and fitness are important for children and young people?**

I think sport and fitness are very important for young people as they make you feel a lot happier and they definitely improve self-esteem! Playing sport is also a great way to socialise with friends and have fun. The healthier you are, the happier you are!

**What is the most memorable goal you ever scored?**

I have two goals that stand out the most in my memory. The first one was away to our rivals, Shamrock Rovers. We won 2-1 and I scored the winning goal. The fans went crazy – it was a special moment for me! The second was away to Drogheda United. I was about 35 yards out from goal and I smashed it into the top corner. I don't score many goals outside the box, so I'll always remember that one.

**What advice would you give to a Sixth Class pupil who would like to be a professional footballer when they grow up?**

The best advice I could give to a young person who wants to be a professional footballer when they grow up is to work hard. Always give 100 per cent, and it's important to enjoy the work too! Listen to what your coaches have to say and work hard.

## And now for some quick-fire questions!

| Question | Answer |
| --- | --- |
| What were your favourite subjects in school? | PE and Maths. |
| What was your worst subject in school? | History. |
| When you were in primary school, what did you want to be when you grew up? | A professional footballer. |
| What is your favourite thing about Christmas? | Seeing my son with his new toys, and spending time with family and friends. |
| What is the best Christmas present you got as a child? | A white stunt bike! |
| If you could meet anyone in the world, dead or alive, who would it be? | My favourite footballer, Lionel Messi. |
| If you had to pick a different sport to be a professional in, what would it be? | Tennis. |
| Finally, do you remember getting *Sonas* in primary school? | I do – vaguely! |

# Phone Code

Ella is texting her friend a riddle. Can you work out what it is?
Use the mobile phone keypad to crack the code.
Each number in the riddle represents one of the letters on that key on the phone.
Remember: You need to work out which letter it is and it's not always the same letter.

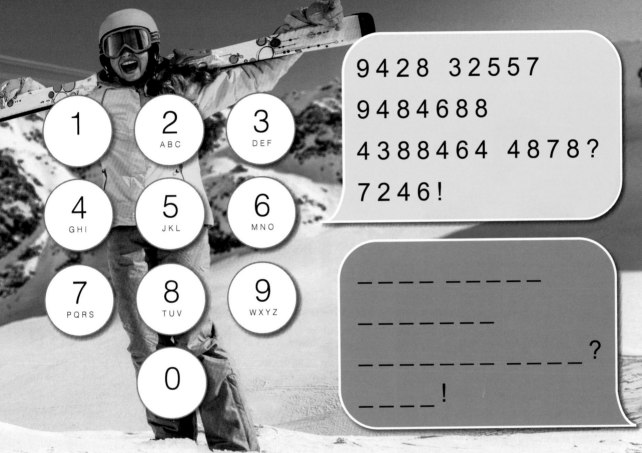

| 1 | 2 ABC | 3 DEF |
|---|---|---|
| 4 GHI | 5 JKL | 6 MNO |
| 7 PQRS | 8 TUV | 9 WXYZ |
| | 0 | |

9428 32557
9484688
4388464 4878?
7246!

\_\_\_\_ \_\_\_\_\_

_____

_____?

\_\_\_\_ !

# Word Pairs

Match the word pairs to find seven games. One word will be left over.
This is the mystery answer.

GO

PURSUIT

CONNECT

BIRDS

CHAIRS

TRIVIAL

MOUSE

FOUR

ANGRY

WHO

HIPPOS

FISH

TRAP

MUSICAL

GUESS

MYSTERY ANSWER:

# Brick in the Wall

How many five-letter words can you find reading down the face of our wall? The letters of each word can only be read downwards on touching bricks, taking one letter only from each line.

# Top Words

Fit all the words from the lists into the grid. Words may run across, backwards, up or down. The completed grid will reveal one word that is not in the lists. Can you discover this mystery answer?

**3 LETTERS**
Car
~~Cur~~
Has
Yew

**5 LETTERS**
Sandy
Tasty
~~Tutor~~

**7 LETTERS**
Carrots
Custody
Hastier
Warrior

**9 LETTERS**
Masterful
~~Patterned~~

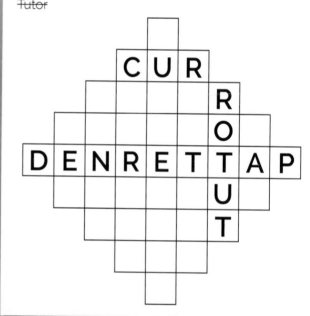

# Wheel Words

Create words of four letters or more using the given letters once only, but always including the middle letter. Do not use proper nouns or plurals. See if you can find the nine-letter word using all the letters.

Good: 10

Very Good: 15

Excellent: 20+

**LEFT RIGHT LEFT**

Santa needs your help to guide him to his first stop. Travelling forward from the Start, follow the directions through the town to find which child he will deliver to first.

JOE'S HOUSE

HARVEY'S HOUSE

AI'S HOUSE

SIENNA'S HOUSE

START

**Directions:**
- 3rd left
- 1st right
- 2nd right
- 1st right
- 2nd left
- 1st right
- 1st left
- 2nd right

*Christmas*

55

# Tracker Wordsearch

Find all the listed words winding backwards and forwards through the spiral of letters. Cross them off as you find them, and the letters left over will spell out one of the things that makes Christmas very exciting.

ANGEL

BAUBLE

BERRIES

BOWS

BRANCHES

BRIGHT

CANDLES

CANDY CANES

DECORATE

ELVES

EVERGREEN

FAIRY

GOLD

GREEN

HANG

HOLLY

HOME

LANTERN

LIGHTS

ORNAMENTS

PINE CONES

PRETTY

SCENT

STAND

STOCKING

TALL

TINSEL

TOYS

TRADITION

MYSTERY ANSWER:

# Rudolf an Fia Rua

Rudolf an fia rua,
Bhí loinnir ar a shrón chomh maith,
Agus dá bhfeicfeá riamh é,
Déarfá linn go raibh sé geal.

Bhíodh na fianna eile
Ag gáire is ag magadh faoi.
Ní ligeadh siad riamh do Rudolf,
Páirt a ghlacadh i gcluichí.

Oíche Nollag cheomhar bhán,
Tháinig San Nioclás,
'Rudolf, le do shrón gheal ghlé,
An rachaidh tú os comhair mo shlé?'

Bhí grá ag na fianna eile dó,
Is bhéic said amach os ard:
'Rudolf, an fia rua,
Nach ortsa a bheas clú is cáil!'

# 50th Anniversary of the Moon Landing

Fifty years ago this year, in July 1969, millions of people all over the world were glued to their television sets. History was about to be made – a human being was about to walk on the Moon for the first time.

## The space race

Competition was fierce between the USA and the Soviet Union in the late 1950s and 1960s. Both countries were determined to be the most successful at exploring space. The Soviet Union took an early lead, becoming the first country to launch a satellite into space with *Sputnik 1* in 1957. They were also the first to send a human being into space: Yuri Gagarin in 1961.

The Americans were determined to be the first to reach the Moon. In 1961, President John F. Kennedy announced that the USA would land an astronaut on the Moon before the decade was over.

At the time, this seemed like a very ambitious plan, and people found it difficult to believe that humans could actually land on the Moon. But NASA worked very hard on developing the technology that would make this possible.

## The journey begins

On 16 July 1969 the spacecraft *Apollo 11* was launched from the Kennedy Space Center in Florida, bound for the Moon. On board were three astronauts – Neil Armstrong, Buzz Aldrin and Michael Collins.

It took another three days for *Apollo 11* to reach the Moon's orbit. On 20 July, Armstrong and Aldrin unlocked the lunar module, the *Eagle*, from the spacecraft and began to descend to the surface of the Moon, leaving Collins on board the main craft.

As they approached the Moon, they realised they were landing in the wrong place, on a much rockier surface than planned. Armstrong took manual control of the *Eagle*. With just 25 seconds of fuel left, he needed to act quickly. He successfully landed the *Eagle* on a smoother surface in a crater known as the Sea of Tranquillity.

## First steps on the Moon

The two men looked out the window of the *Eagle* at the Moon's strange, barren surface. Neil Armstrong climbed down the ladder and became the first human to walk on the Moon, as he said these famous words: 'That's one small step for man, one giant leap for mankind.' Nineteen minutes later, Buzz Aldrin followed him.

Wearing bulky spacesuits and oxygen tanks, the two astronauts planted the USA flag and explored the surface of the Moon. They left behind a plaque bearing a message of peace from Earth. They took photographs and collected samples of rocks and soil to bring back to Earth for examination.

## Over the Moon

Back on planet Earth, millions of people watched this historic moment on TV, as a camera on the *Eagle* beamed back live pictures.

*Apollo 11* returned to Earth on 24 July. The astronauts were given a hero's welcome. They were invited to dinner with President Nixon, appeared on television shows, and had a parade held in their honour.

Over the next few years, several more missions travelled to the Moon, and ten astronauts walked on its surface. The last one was in 1972. No one has walked on the Moon since then.

## Will humans walk on the Moon again?

In March 2019, the USA announced that it would be launching a new mission to the Moon within the next few years, and that the first woman to walk on the Moon would be an American. Watch this space!

### Did you know?

- The Moon is over 405,000 km away from Earth.
- The first journey to the Moon took almost 76 hours.
- The astronauts left behind a disc with messages of peace and goodwill from leaders of 73 countries on Earth.
- The footprints Neil Armstrong and Buzz Aldrin left on the Moon can still be seen there! There is no wind on the moon or erosion to wipe them away.
- Only 12 people have ever walked on the Moon.

FIRST MAN ON THE MOON — UNITED STATES

# Criss Cross

Fit all the words into the spaces. We have put in some words to get you started.

**4 LETTERS**
BOWS
CARS
CATS
DOGS
GOLF
HATS
LIPS

**5 LETTERS**
FROGS
SPOTS
STARS

**6 LETTERS**
ARROWS
BRICKS
HEARTS
LEAVES
RIBBON
SHELLS
SWEETS
WHEELS

**7 LETTERS**
BOTTLES
FLOWERS
PAISLEY
STRIPES

**8 LETTERS**
BIRTHDAY
HEXAGONS
PRESENTS

**9 LETTERS**
CHAMPAGNE
HONEYCOMB

**10 LETTERS**
SNOWFLAKES

# Riddle Ramble

Can you match each riddle with its punchline?

What do you do when an elephant sneezes?

Where do cows go on holidays?

What sleeps with its shoes on?

What is the largest ant in the world?

What sort of stones can't you find in the ocean?

What do you call a banana with wings?

Antarctica!

Get out of the way!

Moo York!

Fruit fly!

A horse!

Dry stones!

# Tracker Wordsearch

Track down all the words relating to snow, winding backwards and forwards through the spiral. Cross them off as you find them and the leftover letters will spell out the mystery answer.

BLIZZARD
CLOUDS
COLD
COLUMNS
CRUST
CRYSTALS
FALL
FLAKES
FLURRY
FREEZING
FROST
GRANULAR
HEXAGONAL
IGLOO
MELT

MOUNTAINS
NEEDLES
PARTICLES
POWDER
PRECIPITATION
SCARF
SCULPTURE
SKIING
SLEET
SLEIGH
SLUSH
SNOWBALL
SNOWMAN
SNOWSHOE
SOFT

MYSTERY ANSWER:

# Spellbound

**ACROSS**

1. Roses and daffodils
5. To fit clothes neatly in a drawer you have to ... them
6. Hurry
8. A fairy uses one of these to grant wishes
11. Tiny mouthfuls of a drink
13. Eskimo house made with blocks of snow
14. Chinese city, ... Kong
16. The man in the Bible who built the Ark
18. Another word for movie
20. Biting insect that lives in an animal's fur
21. Six-sided shape

**DOWN**

1. Pull a sad face
2. Song, ... MacDonald Had A Farm
3. Organ you listen with
4. Japanese seaweed and rice roll
7. What you say when you meet someone
9. Way back in the past, a long time ...
10. Use a spade to make a hole
11. Child, daughter or ...
12. Small green vegetable that grows in a pod
15. The sound a horse makes
17. Pacific, Indian or Atlantic
19. Stir ingredients together to combine them
20. Thick mist that can make it hard to see where you're going

# Words of Wisdom

Wherever you go, go with all your heart.
— *Confucius*

Those who wish to sing, always find a song.
— *Swedish proverb*

There is a magic about you that is all your own.
— *D.M. Dellinger*

Be kind whenever possible. It is always possible.
— *Dalai Lama*

There are two great days in a person's life — the day we are born and the day we discover why.
— *William Barclay*

Never give up: great things take time.
— *Anonymous*

Why fit in when you were born to stand out?
— *Dr. Seuss*

Be a voice, not an echo.
— *Albert Einstein*

Seek magic in every day.
— *Anonymous*

Colour

# World Cup Silver Medallists – Ireland's Hockey Team

In the summer of 2018, a new group of Irish heroes took the country by storm. The women's hockey team, competing in the World Cup in London, won the hearts of the Irish nation with their gritty determination and class.

People who had never watched a hockey match before found themselves glued to their TV screens, cheering for the women as they took on one opponent after another. The excitement grew and reached its high-point when the team made it all the way to the final – the first time an Irish team has ever made it to a World Cup final in any sport.

## The road to the final

Ireland's tournament began with victories over the USA and India, with Deirdre Duke, Shirley McCay and Anna O'Flanagan all scoring valuable goals. The team then lost their third-pool game to England, but they had already qualified for the next round.

In the quarter-final, Ireland drew with India 0-0, and the game went to a penalty shootout. Goalkeeper Ayeisha McFerran was the hero of the hour, saving three out of four penalties as Ireland won 3-1.

Next up was the semi-final against Spain. Anna O'Flanagan scored her second goal of the tournament, but Spain equalised and the match finished 1-1. Another tense penalty shootout followed. Ayeisha McFerran again made some spectacular saves, and Ireland won 3-2.

## World Cup Final

Ireland had made it to the World Cup Final! This was a dream come true for the only amateur team in the competition, and the second lowest ranked side of all those taking part. In the final they came up against a team of full-time professionals, the Netherlands. The Netherlands were firm favourites to win the title, and sadly there was no fairy-tale ending for the Irish team. The final score was 6-0 to the Netherlands.

But the disappointment of losing the final could not take away from Ireland's remarkable success. Winning silver medals in the World Cup was something to treasure.

## The dream team

Each member of the squad played her part in Ireland's amazing achievement. Chloe Watkins described the World Cup as 'one of the best moments of our lives'. Her teammate Deirdre Duke explained, 'I think we had an attitude that we were just going to go out and enjoy it and savour every minute of it, and that allowed us to play with such freedom, and no fear, and there was no expectation, there was nothing to lose.'

Meanwhile, Anna O'Flanagan said, 'We wanted to create a legacy and I believe we've done that.'

No doubt about it!

## National heroes

The team arrived home to a hero's welcome. A civic reception was held in their honour and they were greeted by a crowd of 5,000 supporters on Dame Street in Dublin. President Higgins invited them to visit Áras an Uachtaráin to celebrate their success.

The team went on to be named the RTÉ Sports Team of the Year 2018, as voted by the public. They were also named *Irish Independent* Team of the Year.

Following their amazing progress, they leaped from sixteenth in world rankings to eighth.

## What next?

The team are certainly not content to rest on their laurels: they are hard at work, training for their next big competition.

'It's time to reset – the World Cup was amazing and none of us will forget it, but we have to back it up now. We have to refocus and reset our goals,' said Chloe Watkins.

With their hard work, dedication and determination to dream big, there's no stopping this magnificent Irish team!

### Did you know?

- Ayeisha McFerran was named goalkeeper of the tournament for the World Cup.

- Following their success, money available to fund the team was increased by the Minister for Sport.

- The squad's favourite song to sing together is Mariah Carey's 'All I Want for Christmas Is You'. They sang it on the morning of the World Cup Final – even though it was August!

- Lizzie Colvin revealed that she has asked all 17 of her teammates to be bridesmaids at her wedding!

# Aimsigh na Difríochtaí

Aimsigh deich gcinn de dhifríochtaí idir na pictiúir.

# Maze

Help Charlotte join her friends playing in the snow.

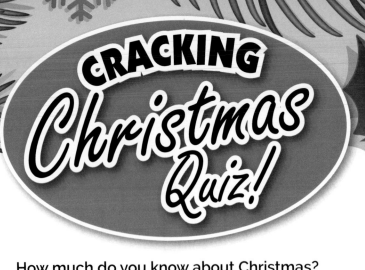

# CRACKING Christmas Quiz!

**How much do you know about Christmas?**
**Take our cracking Christmas quiz to find out!**

1. *The Toy Show* is a special edition of which Irish television programme?

2. In *A Christmas Carol*, Ebenezer Scrooge is visited by three ghosts. Can you name them?

3. Finish this line from a festive poem: 'Twas the night before Christmas, and all through the house, not a creature was stirring, not even a ...'

4. Complete the title of this classic Christmas song: 'I Wish it Could Be Christmas ...'

5. What kind of tree is a Christmas tree?

6. What is the name of Will Ferrell's character in the movie *Elf*?

7. Which one of these is not Santa's reindeer: Comet, Piper, Blitzen?

8. According to the song 'Twelve Days of Christmas', what was sent on the fifth day of Christmas?

9. Complete the title of this Christmas movie: *Miracle on ...*

10. What kind of meat is traditionally eaten for Christmas dinner?

11. What was the name of Ebenezer Scrooge's most loyal employee?

12. Which soft drink company has used Santa in its Christmas advertisements since 1931?

13. Which reindeer's name begins with the letter 'V'?

14. Who played Kevin McCallister in the movie *Home Alone*?

15. What popular Christmas song begins with the words: 'Oh the weather outside is frightful, but the fire is so delightful ...'?

16. What small bird is often featured on Christmas cards?

17. What prickly green plant with red berries is a common decoration at Christmas time?

18. What vegetable is commonly used for a snowman's nose?

19. In which season is Christmas in Australia?

20. According to one classic Christmas song, what does Santa check twice?

21. What is the name of the snowman in the Disney movie *Frozen*?

22. Complete the title of this Christmas carol: 'Away in a ...'

23. Whose birthday do Christians celebrate on Christmas Day?

24. What Dr. Seuss character stole Christmas?

25. What tiny character might you find up on a shelf at Christmas time?

26. Which pop singer originally sang the song 'All I Want For Christmas is You'?

27. Name the animated Christmas movie that starred Tom Hanks.

28. 'Feliz Navidad' means 'Merry Christmas' in which language?

29. What saint is Santa Claus associated with?

30. What is St Stephen's Day known as in the UK?

# Add-Ups

Fill in the blank circles to complete each pyramid. The number in each circle is made up of the sum of the two numbers below. To solve this puzzle it will help to know that there are no zeros in it.

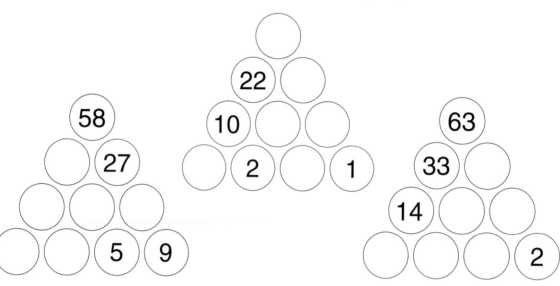

# Set Square

Fill in the missing numbers so that the equations work left to right and top to bottom. Each equation must equal the number indicated at the side or bottom of the grid.

| 1 | + |  | − | 2 | = | 3 |
|---|---|---|---|---|---|---|
| + | ■ | + | ■ | x |  |  |
|  | x |  | − |  | = | 5 |
| + | ■ | − | ■ | − |  |  |
| 10 | − | 8 | + |  | = | 8 |
| = |  | = |  | = |  |  |
| 13 |  | 2 |  | 8 |  |  |

| 7 | x |  | x |  | = | 70 |
|---|---|---|---|---|---|---|
| + | ■ | + | ■ | − |  |  |
|  | − | 1 | − |  | = | 1 |
| − | ■ | + | ■ | + |  |  |
| 10 | x | 6 | − |  | = | 53 |
| = |  | = |  | = |  |  |
| 6 |  | 8 |  | 10 |  |  |

# Fill In

Fit all the snow words into the spaces. We have put some in to help you start.
The letters in the coloured squares will spell out the mystery answer.

**3 LETTERS**
AIR
ICY

**4 LETTERS**
COLD

**5 LETTERS**
BOOTS
~~HEAVY~~
LIGHT

**6 LETTERS**
ALPINE
CLOUDS
FLUFFY

FREEZE
FROSTY
POWDER
~~WINTER~~

**7 LETTERS**
FALLING

**8 LETTERS**
CRYSTALS

**9 LETTERS**
SNOWSHOES

**13 LETTERS**
PRECIPITATION

MYSTERY ANSWER: _____

# Quiz Quest

All the answers to the clues are in the boxes, either as a word or picture.
Solve all the clues and cross off the boxes. One word will be left over.
This is the mystery answer.

## CLUES

- Icy sculpture that you might make with your friends
- Slip these over your hands to keep them from getting cold
- Large white animal that hunts seals and lives in the Arctic Circle
- They make presents in a workshop at the North Pole
- You might hang this beside your bed in the hope of receiving presents
- Part of a house where you'll find logs burning to keep everyone warm
- Jolly fellow who comes down the chimney to deliver gifts
- This is a device used to tell you the temperature
- Type of biscuit that's usually made in the shape of a person
- Along with milk, you might leave these out as an offering on Christmas Eve
- Dasher, Dancer or Rudolph
- Hot chocolate drink
- The leaves of this shrub are used as a Christmas decoration
- It can be used to slide down snowy hills

MYSTERY ANSWER: _____

# Happy New Year!

People around the world celebrate the new year in lots of interesting ways – here are just some of them!

## Spain
In Spain there is a custom of eating twelve grapes, one on each stroke of midnight. This is supposed to bring good luck for each of the twelve months of the new year!

## Scotland
New Year is known as Hogmanay in Scotland and it's one of the biggest celebrations of the year. One of the most important traditions is 'first footing'. This means being the first visitor to enter a home after midnight. It is especially lucky if this person is a tall, dark-haired man carrying a piece of coal!

## Greece
Greek people hang onions on their front doors as a symbol of rebirth for the new year. They also play cards on New Year's Eve, either at home or in cafes.

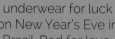

## Brazil
People wear special underwear for luck on New Year's Eve in Brazil. Red for love, white for peace and yellow for money!

## Denmark
In Denmark people stand on chairs then jump off them at midnight, so they can 'leap' into the new year together! They also throw old crockery at the doors of their friends and neighbours to banish bad spirits.

## Ecuador
Paper scarecrows are burned in Ecuador to bring luck for the new year.

## Macedonia
A second New Year celebration is held in Macedonia on 14 January, the Orthodox new year. Children receive presents from their relatives.

## Finland

In Finland a game is played to make predictions for the year ahead by dropping melted tin into a bucket of water to see what shape it forms. A heart or a ring means you will find love, a horse or a ship means you will travel, and a pig means you will be rich! But if the tin breaks into pieces, that means bad luck for the next year.

## Switzerland

In Switzerland there is a tradition of dropping ice cream on the floor, to symbolise riches for the new year.

## Japan

Buddhist temples in Japan ring their bells 108 times to banish the sins of the old year.

## Philippines

In the Philippines, circles or discs are very important shapes in New Year celebrations, as they represent coins. People wear clothes with polka dots and eat round fruits for luck, in particular grapes.

## Wales

The old tradition in parts of rural Wales was for children to call from door to door bringing skewered apples decorated with cloves and sprigs of evergreen. In return, the children received a 'Calennig' or New Year's gift of coins.

## Louisiana, USA

In Louisiana people eat a special stew made with black-eyed peas and cabbage, which represents health and wealth for the year ahead.

## Yorkshire, England

An old tradition in Yorkshire refers to rabbits! As the clock is about to strike midnight, you are supposed to say: 'Black rabbits, black rabbits, black rabbits!' Then, as the clock chimes 12, you say: 'White rabbits, white rabbits, white rabbits!' This apparently brings good luck.

# Crack the Code

Can you work out this Christmas message? Look at the pictures and write the first letter of each word in the boxes below.

# Broken Hearted

Mend these broken hearts to form the names of ten couples who carved their names on a tree, only to find it chopped down and split in half. There's only one way to get all ten couples together correctly.

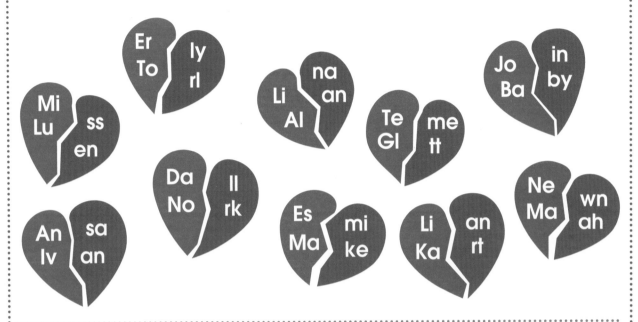

# Star Words

In this puzzle you will find the names of different flowers hidden inside each of the clues. When you've finished, the stars reading top to bottom will spell the mystery answer. We've given you the first answer to start.

Broccoli lyrics — ☆L I L Y

Chair island — ◯ ◯ ☆

Tutu lipstick — ◯ ◯ ☆ ◯ ◯

Frypan system — ◯ ☆ ◯ ◯ ◯

Torch ideas — ◯ ◯ ☆ ◯ ◯ ◯

MYSTERY ANSWER: _____

# COMPETITION TIME

**Happy Christmas to all our *Sonas* readers!**

It's competition time again and we are giving away lots of fantastic prizes. All you have to do is answer the following four questions and you could win a prize. The answer to Question 1 can be found in the article 'The Late Late Toy Show'. You'll find the answer to Question 2 in the article '50th Anniversary of the Moon Landing'. The answer to Question 3 is in 'Swimming in a Sea of Plastic – Ten Things You Should Know', while the answer to Question 4 is in 'Happy New Year!'.

Question 1: Who was the first host of *The Late Late Toy Show*?

Question 2: Who was the first person to walk on the Moon?

Question 3: How many plastic bottles are bought around the world every minute?

Question 4: In Greece, what do people hang on their front doors to celebrate the New Year?

For your chance to win, write your answers on the competition entry form on page 77 with your name, parent's telephone number or email address, and your school name, address and roll number.

The closing date is 10 January 2020. Winners and prizes will be published on our website **www.folens.ie** and announced on social media by 31 January 2020.
*Images for illustration purpose only. Full competition terms and details are available on Folens.ie.*

# ENTRY FORM
# SONAS 2019

Pupil's name:

Parent's telephone number or email address:

School roll number:

School name and address:

Answer to Question 1:

Answer to Question 2:

Answer to Question 3:

Answer to Question 4:

**Post your competition entry form to:**

*Sonas* 2019 Competition

Folens Publishers
Hibernian Industrial Estate
Greenhills Road
Tallaght
Dublin 24

Or you can email your answers with your name, parent's telephone number or email address, and your school name, address and roll number to **sonas@folens.ie** (please put 'Sonas Main Competition' in the subject line).

The closing date is 10 January 2020. If you have any queries about the competition, check out **www.folens.ie**. The winners and prizes will be published on our website **www.folens.ie** and announced on social media by 31 January 2020. Good luck!

# ?Solutions??

## Page 4 – Last Word Standing
Mystery Answer: Holiday.

## Page 4 – Chainletters
Solution: Overindulging.

## Page 4 – What's What
1. ABC. 2. Elf. 3. Jig. 4. Ash. 5. MSG. 6. Off.
7. Gun. 8. Ply. Solution: Blissful.

## Page 5 – Cé mhéad?
A. 2. B. 1. C. 3. D. 5.

## Page 9 – Christmas Time

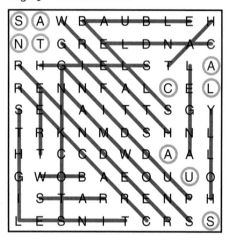

Mystery Answer: Santa Claus.

## Page 12 – Phone Code
What do sea monsters eat?
Fish and ships!

## Page 12 – Word Pairs
Advent calendar. Candy cane. Jingle bells.
Mince pies. North Pole. Santa Claus.
Silent Night. Mystery Answer: Tree.

## Page 13 – Colour Sudoku

| 4 | 7 | 2 | 9 | 1 | 3 | 6 | 8 | 5 |
|---|---|---|---|---|---|---|---|---|
| 9 | 5 | 3 | 6 | 4 | 8 | 7 | 1 | 2 |
| 1 | 8 | 6 | 2 | 5 | 7 | 4 | 9 | 3 |
| 7 | 6 | 1 | 8 | 2 | 9 | 3 | 5 | 4 |
| 8 | 9 | 4 | 7 | 3 | 5 | 2 | 6 | 1 |
| 3 | 2 | 5 | 1 | 6 | 4 | 9 | 7 | 8 |
| 2 | 4 | 9 | 5 | 8 | 6 | 1 | 3 | 7 |
| 5 | 3 | 7 | 4 | 9 | 1 | 8 | 2 | 6 |
| 6 | 1 | 8 | 3 | 7 | 2 | 5 | 4 | 9 |

## Page 13 – Colour Sudoku

| 5 | 9 | 2 | 3 | 8 | 7 | 4 | 6 | 1 |
|---|---|---|---|---|---|---|---|---|
| 6 | 1 | 8 | 2 | 4 | 9 | 5 | 3 | 7 |
| 3 | 7 | 4 | 6 | 5 | 1 | 2 | 9 | 8 |
| 4 | 6 | 5 | 9 | 2 | 8 | 1 | 7 | 3 |
| 7 | 3 | 1 | 5 | 6 | 4 | 8 | 2 | 9 |
| 2 | 8 | 9 | 1 | 7 | 3 | 6 | 5 | 4 |
| 9 | 2 | 7 | 8 | 1 | 6 | 3 | 4 | 5 |
| 8 | 4 | 6 | 7 | 3 | 5 | 9 | 1 | 2 |
| 1 | 5 | 3 | 4 | 9 | 2 | 7 | 8 | 6 |

## Pages 14 & 15 – Fact or Fiction
1. Fact. 2. Fiction: *The Late Late Toy Show* first hit our screens in 1975. 3. Fact: The African continent is much larger than most maps show, measuring over 30 million km². 4. Fact. 5. Fact: Saffron is so expensive that it is sold by the gram. It costs approximately €10 per gram at the supermarket. 6. Fiction: Ankara is the capital of Turkey. 7. Fiction: The Rubik's cube was first known as 'The Magic Cube'. 8. Fact. 9. Fiction: 'Safari' means 'journey' in Swahili. 10. Fact. 11. Fiction: A Great Dane holds the record. 12. Fact. 13. Fiction: A group of giraffes is known as a 'tower'. 14. Fact. 15. Fiction: The oldest zoo in the world is located in the grounds of the famous Schönbrunn Palace in Vienna, Austria. It was founded in 1752. 16. Fiction: 'Áras an Uachtaráin' means 'House of the President'. 17. Fact: Ireland has over 1,000 km of motorway, whereas New Zealand has under 400 km of motorway. 18. Fact. 19. Fact: A pumpkin is a fruit because it is a product of the seed-bearing structure of flowering plants. Vegetables, on the other hand, are the edible portion of plants such as leaves, stems, roots, bulbs and flowers. 20. Fiction: Murphy is Ireland's most common surname.

## Page 16 – Irish Word Match
Bell – Cloigín, Candle – Coinneal, Christmas Tree – Crann Nollag, Christmas card – Cárta Nollag, Pudding – Maróg, Christmas – Nollaig, Cracker – Pléascóg, Reindeer – Réinfhia, Snow – Sneachta, Stocking – Stoca, Chimney – Simléar, Presents – Bronntanais, Gloves – Lámhainní, Sleigh – Carr sleamhnáin, Holly – Cuileann, Star – Réalta.

## Page 17 – Riddle Me This!
1. The person was walking. 2. A lantern.
3. The word 'Toronto'.
4. They are part of a set of triplets.
5. The woman's name is 'There'.
6. Soap. 7. The letter 't'. 8. Choice.

## Page 19 – Findaword

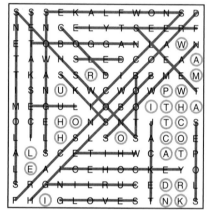

Mystery Answer: Warm up with a hot chocolate drink.

## Page 19 – Spellbound

## Page 23 – Book Quiz
1. Wells and Wong Detective Society.
2. *War Horse*. 3. *The Midnight Gang*.
4. Zoe Sugg. 5. *The Forever Court*. 6. An elf.
7. When the seeker catches the golden snitch
8. *Hetty Feather*. 9. St Clare's. 10. Amy.
11. *Alice in Wonderland*. 12. The Lotterys.
13. *Five Children and It*. 14. Skulduggery Pleasant. 15. John Green. 16. Veronica Roth.
17. Aslan. 18. Cora Staunton. 19. Peeta.
20. *Wonder*.

## Page 24 – Letter Scramble
1. Bonfire. 2. Tinsel.

## Page 28 – Broken Hearted
Fritz & Mitzi, Jerry & Patty, Barry & Grace, Raoul & Carol, Keith & Maria, Shane & Peggy, Andre & Renee, Gavin & Megan, Bryan & Karen, Wally & Agnes.

## Page 28 – Memory Game Questions
1. No, 2. 3, 3. Red and white, 4. Yes, 5. Two, 6. Ice skates, 7. Yes, 8. Red.

## Page 34 – Aimsigh na Focail

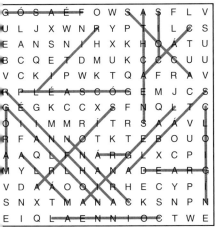

## Page 35 – Hexoku

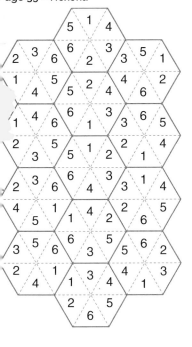

## Pages 38 & 39 – Christmas Findaword

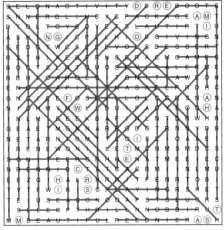

Mystery Answer: Dreaming of a white Christmas.

## Page 42 – Last Word Standing
Mystery Answer: Snowman.

## Page 42 – Chainletters
Solution: Spectacularly.

## Page 42 – What's What
1. Spa. 2. Fad. 3. Art. 4. Ban. 5. Odd. 6. Her. 7. Ash. Solution: Parades.

## Page 43 – The Sports Quiz
1. Tokyo. 2. Shamrock Rovers. 3. Offaly. 4. True. 5. Athletics. 6. Wembley, London. 7. Deuce. 8. Golf. 9. Sixty-eight. 10. Basketball. 11. Cork. 12. George Best. 13. Camogie. 14. Peter Stringer. 15. Walsh. 16. Cricket. 17. True. 18. Michael Phelps. 19. Running, swimming and cycling. 20. New Zealand.

## Page 44 – Maze

## Page 45 – Aimsigh na Difríochtaí

## Page 53 – Phone Code
What falls without getting hurt? Rain!

## Page 53 – Word Pairs
Angry Birds. Connect Four. Go Fish. Guess Who. Mouse Trap. Musical Chairs. Trivial Pursuit. Mystery Answer: Hippos.

## Page 54 – Brick in the Wall
Brake, brand, chart, choke, chore, craft, shaft, share, shore, short, stake, stand, stoke, store.

## Page 54 – Top Words

Mystery Answer: Safer.

## Page 54 – Wheel Words
Emit, item, lest, list, lost, meet, melt, mete, milt, mist, mite, mitt, most, mote, omit, silt, site, slit, slot, stem, stet, teem, test, tile, tilt, time, toil, tome, tote; elite, emote, islet, istle, metis, metol, moist, motel, motet, sleet, smelt, smite, smote, steel, stele, stile, stilt, stole, title, totem; mettle, mottle, settle, toilet; mottles. Nine-letter word: mistletoe.

## Page 55 – Left, Right, Left

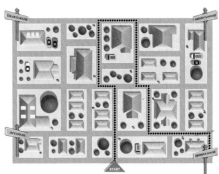

Solution: Sienna's house.

## Page 56 – Tracker Wordsearch
Mystery Answer: Presents.

## Page 60 – Criss Cross

## Page 60 – Riddle Ramble

What do you do when an elephant sneezes?
Get out of the way!

Where do cows go on holidays?
Moo York!

What sleeps with its shoes on?
A horse!

What is the largest ant in the world?
Antarctica!

What sort of stones can't you find in the ocean?
Dry stones!

What do you call a banana with wings?
Fruit fly!

## Page 61 – Tracker Wordsearch
Mystery Answer: Warm coat.

## Page 61 – Spellbound

## Page 66 – Aimsigh na Difríochtaí

## Page 67 – Maze

## Pages 68 & 69 – Cracking Christmas Quiz

1. *The Late Late Show*. 2. The Ghost of
Christmas Past, the Ghost of Christmas
Present and the Ghost of Christmas Yet to
Come. 3. Mouse. 4. Every Day. 5. Fir tree.
6. Buddy. 7. Piper. 8. Five gold rings.
9. 34th Street. 10. Turkey. 11. Bob Cratchit.
12. Coca-Cola. 13. Vixen. 14. Macaulay Culkin.
15. Let It Snow. 16. A robin. 17. Holly. 18. A carrot.
19. Summer. 20. A list. 21. Olaf. 22. Manger.
23. Jesus Christ. 24. The Grinch. 25. An elf.
26. Mariah Carey. 27. *The Polar Express*.
28. Spanish. 29. Saint Nicholas. 30. Boxing Day.

## Page 70 – Add-Ups

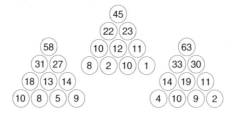

## Page 70 – Set Square

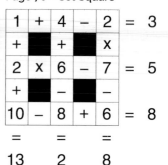

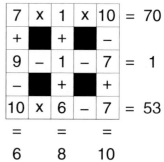

## Page 71 – Fill In

Mystery Answer: Frozen.

## Page 71 – Quiz Quest

Snowman, Gloves, Polar bear, Elves, Stocking,
Fireplace, Santa Claus, Thermometer,
Gingerbread, Cookies, Reindeer, Cocoa,
Mistletoe, Sleigh.
Mystery Answer: Carols.

## Page 74 – Crack the Code

On the first day of Christmas my true love sent
to me,  A partridge in a pear tree.

## Page 75 – Broken Hearted

Mimi & Luke, Erin & Toby, Lisa & Alan,
Tess & Glen, Joan & Bart, Anna & Ivan,
Dawn & Noah, Esme & Matt, Lily & Karl,
Nell & Mark.

## Page 75 – Star Words

Lily, Iris, Tulip, Pansy, Orchid.
Mystery Answer: Lilac.